IAN FLEMING

# ON HER MAJESTY'S SECRET SERVICE

JONATHAN CAPE
THIRTY BEDFORD SQUARE
LONDON

DOCTOR NO

by

IAN FLEMING

Copy for headlines

GOLDFINGER

by Ian Fleming
author of Casino Royale, Dr No, etc.

Goldfinger, the man who loved gold, said, "Mr Bond, it was a most evil day for you when you first crossed my path. If you had then found an oracle to consult, the oracle would have said to you "Mr Bond, keep away from Mr Auric Goldfinger. He is a most powerful man. If Mr Goldfinger wished to crush you, he would only have to turn over in his sleep to do so"."

With the icily precision of Fate, this, Ian Fleming's longest narrative of secret service adventure, brings James Bond to grips with the most powerful criminal the world has ever known – Goldfinger, the man who had planned the "Crime de la Crime".

Le Chiffre, Mr Big, Sir Hugo Drax, Jack Spang, Rosa Klebb, Doctor No – and now, the seventh adversary, a Goliath of crime – GOLDFINGER!

300 pp. Crown 8vo. 15s. net

[March 23]

# FOR YOUR EYES ONLY
## IAN FLEMING + JAMES BOND

## BEN MACINTYRE

BLOOMSBURY

# FOR YOUR EYES ONLY

BY THE SAME AUTHOR
The Napoleon of Crime
Josiah the Great
Forgotten Fatherland
A Foreign Field
Agent Zigzag

Published by Bloomsbury USA, New York
Distributed to the trade by Macmillan

LIBRARY OF CONGRESS CATALOGING IN PUBLICATION DATA HAS BEEN APPLIED FOR.

ISBN-13: 978-1-59691-544-2
ISBN-10: 1-59691-544-7
10 9 8 7 6 5 4 3 2 1

Book design and illustrations by Grade Design Consultants, London
www.gradedesign.com

Printed in Great Britain by Butler and Tanner, Frome and London

# CONTENTS

# AUTHOR'S NOTE

This book, published to coincide with a major exhibition at the Imperial War Museum in London, is a homage to Ian Fleming on the centenary of the author's birth, and a celebration of James Bond, his greatest creation. It is not a biography of Ian Fleming – others, notably John Pearson and Andrew Lycett, have already performed that task admirably – nor is it a 'biography' of James Bond, for that, too, has been written. It does not purport to be a comprehensive guide to the James Bond phenomenon (for this, I recommend Henry Chancellor's official companion). Rather, it is a personal investigation into the intersection of two lives, one real and one fictional.

As a journalist and writer of non-fiction, I have always been intrigued by the factual origins of fiction. In previous books, I went in search of the nineteenth-century criminal Adam Worth, the model for Professor Moriarty in the Sherlock Holmes tales, and Josiah Harlan, an adventurer who would win literary immortality in Rudyard Kipling's short story 'The Man Who Would Be King'. All novelists find inspiration in reality, but Ian Fleming, more than any writer I know, anchored the imagined world of James Bond to the people, things and places he knew. Espionage is itself a shadowy trade between truth and untruth, a complex interweaving of imagination, deception and reality. As a former officer in naval intelligence, Fleming thought like a spy, and wrote like one. This book is an attempt to explore a remarkable double life and to establish, as nearly as possible, where the real world of Ian Fleming ended and the fictional world of James Bond begins.

Ben Macintyre, April 2008

PREVIOUS

Sean Connery and Ian Fleming on the film set of *Dr No*, 1962.

Ian Fleming poses by a Bentley, similar to Bond's first car, the battleship-grey 1933 4.5-litre Bentley convertible he drives in *Casino Royale*.

Fleming at the card table. 'The same cries of victory and defeat, the same dedicated faces, the same smell of tobacco and drama. For Bond, who loved to gamble, it was the most exciting spectacle in the world.' (*Moonraker*)

OPPOSITE

The film poster for *Dr No*, the first James Bond film, released in 1962 and starring Sean Connery as James Bond, Ursula Andress as Honey (Honeychile in the book) Ryder, and Joseph Wiseman as Dr No.

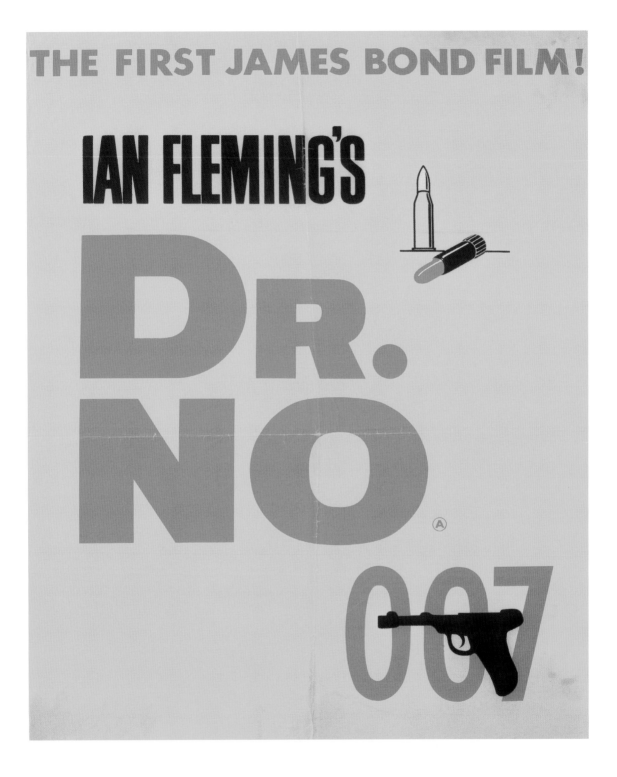

# 001

'THE SCENT AND SMOKE
AND SWEAT OF A CASINO...'

## 001
'The scent and smoke and sweat of a casino…'

One morning in February 1952, in a holiday hideaway on the island of Jamaica, a middle-aged British journalist sat down at his desk and set about creating a fictional secret agent, a character that would go on to become one of the most successful, enduring and lucrative creations in literature. The circumstances were not immediately auspicious. Ian Fleming had never written a novel before, though he had done much else. He had tried his hand at banking, stockbroking and working as a newspaper correspondent. As a young man of English privilege, he had toyed with the idea of being a soldier, or a diplomat, but neither had worked out. Only during the war, working in the Intelligence Division of the Royal Navy, had he found a task – as an officer in naval intelligence dreaming up schemes to bamboozle the enemy – worthy of his vivid imagination. But by 1952, the excitement of the war was just a memory. He had settled into a job as a writer and manager on the *Sunday Times*, a role that involved some enjoyable travel, a little work and a lot of golf, women and lunch. Born to wealth and status, Ian Fleming found his existence undemanding but unsatisfying. Even his best friends would have snorted at the notion that he was destined for immortality.

This, then, was the man who, after a morning swim to wash out the hangover of the night before, hunched over the desk in his Jamaican home 'Goldeneye' and began to type, using six fingers, on his elderly Royal portable typewriter. The opening line, after several amendments and corrections, would read: 'The scent and smoke and sweat of a casino are nauseating at three in the morning…' Fleming wrote fast, the words pouring out at the rate of two thousand a day, crammed into the space between dawn and the first cocktail, a great rush of creativity conceived in haste and a miasma of tobacco smoke.

A month after he had started writing, Fleming tapped out the words '…"the bitch is dead now".' *Casino Royale* was complete, and James Bond was born.

Daniel Craig's blood-stained shirt from the 2006 film of *Casino Royale*.

OVERLEAF
Goldeneye, the holiday home on the north shore of Jamaica purchased by Ian Fleming after the war, where he would write the Bond books.

Like the character he had created, Ian Fleming was a great deal more complex than he seemed on first acquaintance. Beneath the sybaritic exterior, Fleming was a driven man, intensely observant, with an internal sense of romance and drama that belied his public languor and occasional cynicism. He pretended not to take his books too seriously – 'the pillow fantasies of an adolescent mind' was how he later described them – but he approached the craft of thriller-writing with the precision of a professional, and he knew, instinctively, exactly what he was doing. He wrote for many reasons: to take his mind off his impending marriage to Ann Rothermere; increasingly, to prove to her somewhat snooty literary friends that he was a genuine novelist; to emulate his brother, the successful travel writer Peter Fleming; and to stop his friend and neighbour in Jamaica, Noël Coward, from badgering him to get on and 'write his bloody book'. He also wrote to make money, preferably in large quantities. Fleming liked money (his lifestyle demanded it), and never felt he had quite enough. James Bond would soon help to put that right.

However, for all Fleming's apparent insouciance, this was no mere money-making venture, but an expression and extension of an extraordinary man. Bond is, in part, Fleming. The exploits of 007 grew directly out of Fleming's knowledge of wartime intelligence and espionage; they shared similar tastes and attitudes towards women; they even looked similar. Fleming would teasingly refer to the Bond books as 'autobiography'. Like every good journalist, Fleming was a magpie, collecting material avidly and continuously: names, places, plots, gadgets, faces, restaurant menus and phrases; details from reality that would then be translated into fiction. He once remarked: 'Everything I write has a precedent in truth.' Fleming's research extended to his own personality, which would find expression in a handsome, attractive and conflicted secret agent.

But Bond is also, in part, what Fleming was not. He was the fantasy of what Fleming would like to have been – indeed, what every Englishman raised on Bulldog Drummond and wartime derring-do would like to have been. Bond is a grown-up romantic fairy tale, a promise that Britain, having triumphed in the World War, was still a force to be reckoned with in the dull chill of the Cold War. In the grim austerity of postwar Britain, here was a man dining on champagne and caviar, enjoying guiltless sex, glamorous foreign travel, and an apparently unlimited expense account.

This was the Bond recipe: part imagination and part truth; part Ian Fleming and part his alter ego; fiction based on fact, with a dash of journalism. This thriller cocktail was as heady and intoxicating as the weapons-grade martini James Bond orders in *Casino Royale*: 'Three measures of Gordon's, one of vodka, half a measure of Kina Lillet. Shake it very well until it's ice cold, then add a large thick slice of lemon-peel.' Kina Lillet was a particularly bitter wine-based aperitif laced with quinine from the bark of the South American cinchona tree, or 'kina kina'; vodka mixed with gin is a particularly lethal combination. Drinking one of these Bond cocktails is a little like reading one's first Bond novel: it leaves you reeling, light-headed and faintly guilty, but keen for another.

*Casino Royale* contains many of the ingredients that explain why Bond would go on to conquer the world: beautiful, externally tough but emotionally vulnerable women; a glamorous setting; a repulsive villain; cold-blooded communist killers; sex, violence and luxury. But it is the character of Bond – established in the first novel and hardly altered thereafter – that explains the enduring appeal of the world Fleming forged: tough, resourceful, quintessentially British, but also, as Fleming intended, empty – the blunt instrument of the British secret service, a blank slate for the reader to write on.

Thirteen more Bond books would follow *Casino Royale*. By the time of his death, just twelve years later, Ian Fleming had sold more than forty million copies, and the first two Bond films had been made, to acclaim, giving birth to a multi-billion-dollar industry that expands with every passing year. Today, more than half the world's population has seen at least one Bond film. Ann, Fleming's wife, would nickname him 'Thunderbeatle', as rich and celebrated as the Beatles themselves. Bond not only outlived Fleming, but continues to be reborn: new films, new books authorised by the Fleming estate, new spoofs. Every age gets the Bond it needs. He is updated with new attitudes to sex, smoking and alcohol, and remodelled with fresh tailoring, new enemies and ever more imaginative gadgets. The film Bond evolved in different ways from Fleming's creation, taking on the characteristics of actors as different as Sean Connery, George Lazenby, Roger Moore, Timothy Dalton, Pierce Brosnan and now Daniel Craig. In the books, Bond kills sparingly, while on screen the carnage is often staggering. Fleming's Bond is vulnerable, prey to nerves and even fear, whereas on screen he barely bleeds, let alone psychologically. Yet the essential Bond is the same, the brand eternal: a sardonic, stylish, seductive Englishman, with a licence not just to kill, but to perform every feat that an armchair Bond can imagine.

Back in 1952, having finished what he called his 'oafish opus', Fleming stuck the sixty-thousand-word manuscript in his briefcase and for some time showed it to no one. One of the first to read it, a former girlfriend, Clare Blanchard, told him waspishly: 'If you must publish it, for heaven's sake do it under a different name' – with hindsight one of the worst pieces of advice in literary history. Fleming claimed the writing of this 'thriller thing' had been easy, the distraction of a few hours, dashed off with 'half his brain'. He would maintain this airy attitude to the end, insisting that *Casino Royale* could be boiled down to a few key elements: 'I extracted them from my wartime memories,' he remarked, 'dolled them up, attached a hero, a villain and a heroine, and there was the book.'

This nonchalance was, we can be sure, the purest bluff, something that Fleming, as a lifelong card-player and former expert in naval intelligence, was very good at. He may have pretended to dismiss his creation, and play down its literary merit, but he must have known that he had written a remarkable book, albeit remarkably fast. The idea for Bond had been gestating in his mind, and his personality, for at least a decade. Back in 1944, as the war reached its climax, Fleming had told a friend in deep earnestness: 'I am going to write the spy story to end all spy stories.'

And that is exactly what he did.

The title page of the manuscript of *Dr No*.

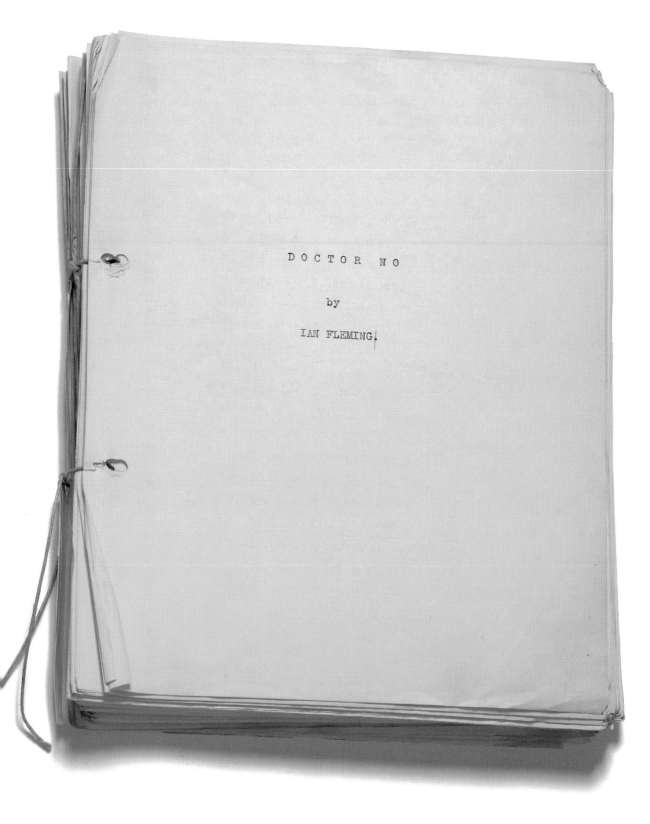

DOCTOR NO

by

IAN FLEMING

# 002

## THE LIFE:
## SMELLING BATTLE FROM AFAR

## 002
### The Life: Smelling Battle from Afar

Ian Lancaster Fleming: even his name had an imagined romance sewn into it, for his mother liked to claim descent from John of Gaunt, the fourteenth-century Duke of Lancaster and the rich and powerful son of Edward III. Whether this claim to medieval royal ancestry contained any truth is unclear, and perhaps unimportant, for Fleming family myth was a powerful force, and an important element in the genetic recipe that made up James Bond.

    The Flemings were certainly wealthy and well connected. On the eve of Ian's birth, they represented the epitome of the Edwardian moneyed class, though the money was new – barely two generations old – a fact that may explain Ian's eternal preoccupation with the stuff. His grandfather, Robert, born in a Dundee slum, had made a vast fortune through American railroads and other shrewd investments, with which he had built a forty-four-room Gothic mansion in Oxfordshire, and instant respectability. The Flemings were tweedy, hearty, thrifty and vigorous, dedicated to outdoor pursuits and blood sports. Besides money and social cachet, Robert Fleming bequeathed to his sons, including the eldest, Valentine (Ian's father), a taste for hard work, a certain Presbyterian rigidity, and a family motto that emphasised action over reflection: 'Let the deed *shaw* [show].'

    Ian Fleming's parents might have stepped straight from a sepia photograph illustrating the twilight of the Edwardian era in all its doomed romance. Val Fleming was a rising star in the Conservative Party, a friend of Winston Churchill and a pillar of the landed squirearchy. A pure product of Eton and Oxford, he was handsome, gentle, intelligent and seemingly marked for success. His wife, Eve Ste Croix Rose, was equally beautiful, but bohemian, socially ambitious, wilful and artistic, with a domineering personality.

    Ian, their second son, was born, on 28 May 1908, into a world of great privilege and great expectations. The first eight years of his life were idyllic, his main hurdle being how to make an impression beneath the shadow of his elder brother Peter, who was, in almost every

IAN LANCASTER FLEMING

The Fleming family coat of arms and motto: 'Let the deed shaw' (show).

OPPOSITE
Peter and Ian Fleming, the two eldest of the four Fleming sons. Their relationship was close, mutually supportive and affectionately competitive.

OVERLEAF
Evelyn Beatrice Ste Croix Fleming (née Rose), Ian Fleming's beautiful, domineering mother, who was known to the young Fleming boys, intriguingly, as 'M'.

Valentine Fleming, Fleming's adored father, who was killed in action while serving on the Western Front in 1917.

respect, the sort of ideal child every parent longs for, and younger brothers traditionally detest. Peter was precocious, effortlessly brilliant and, if you happened to be a brother a year younger, a focus of rapt hero-worship and a permanent reminder of inadequacy. Two more brothers followed, Richard and Michael. A friend described the self-confident Fleming sons as an intimidating, charmed unit of 'strong, handsome, black-haired, blue-eyed boys'. There were the traditional nannies, and the traditionally brutal prep school, Durnford, an institution near Swanage which epitomised the strange British faith in bad food, plenty of Latin and beating from an early age. 'My coff has grown to whoping coff now,' Ian wrote to his mother stoically, at the age of seven. 'Please dont tell Mister Pellatt [the headmaster] cause just this morning he said that nun of us had coffs. I am afraid I do not like school very much.' In fact the regime seems to have made Ian no more miserable or ill than anyone else. The headmaster's wife read to the pupils from contemporary classics of boys' adventure: John Buchan's Richard Hannay stories, Fu Man Chu, *The Prisoner of Zenda* and later Bulldog Drummond, tales of strange and evil

Ian and Peter on the terrace
of their home in Oxfordshire,
near where their grandfather
had built a huge Gothic
mansion as the family seat.

RIGHT
Ian with his mother on
the beach. In his writings,
Fleming recalled his
childhood beach holidays
with a deep and nostalgic
affection, which he
transferred to James Bond.

foreigners, stiff upper lips, and knock-out upper-cuts. This was the sort of story Fleming loved and, many years later, would write in an updated form.

But long before that, Fleming would find a real-life action hero tragically close to home. In 1914, Valentine Fleming had headed to the Western Front as an officer with the Oxfordshire Hussars. His moving letters to a friend and fellow officer, Winston Churchill, describing the pitted and charred landscape of the battlefront, suggest that the literary skills of both Peter and Ian were at least partly inherited. In May 1917, after a war of distinguished gallantry, Major Valentine Fleming, DSO, was killed in the trenches by shellfire.

The Fleming boys idolised their father (nicknamed 'Mokie', on account of his 'Smokey' pipe), and after his death he became an unattainable symbol of chivalry and moral goodness. In their nightly prayers, the boys would entreat the Almighty to 'Make me more like Mokie.' The desire to emulate this military father-hero would run through the lives of every Fleming son, but perhaps most notably in Ian, and his fictional counterpart. It does not do to over-psychoanalyse James

BELOW

Ian and Peter's elaborately decorated Christmas stockings, showing early signs of the creativity that both would demonstrate in later life.

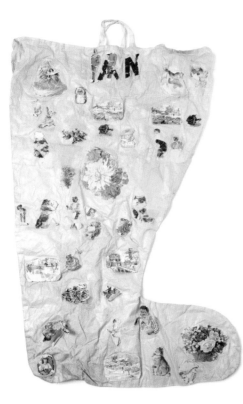

Bond, but perhaps this tragedy offers some clue to 007's fatherless reverence for 'M', to the way that every villain lectures Bond as if speaking to a wayward little boy, and to the exaggerated respect Fleming showed towards older men for the rest of his life. Churchill himself wrote an obituary of Val Fleming, mourning the death of this bright hope with such a 'lovable and charming personality', and a signed, framed copy of the eulogy was kept by Ian Fleming as a treasure throughout his life. 'He was a man of thoughtful and tolerant opinions, which were not the less strongly or clearly held because they were not loudly or frequently asserted.'

Fleming would always retain what he called a 'mysterious affection' for Eton, the elite British public school he attended from 1921. Peter had, of course, preceded him, blazing a trail of athletic and academic success that Ian veered away from with all the energy and wilfulness a second son could muster. Ian was often in trouble, frequently beaten by his sadistic housemaster, and notably deficient in most aspects of his schoolwork. He also discovered girls, and lost his virginity in a box at the Royalty Kinema, Windsor – an experience

BELOW LEFT

Ian Fleming competing in the long jump at Eton. He would twice win the title of *Victor Ludorum*, athletics champion, a feat of which he was intensely proud.

BELOW RIGHT

Fleming (*second from right*) attending a dining club at Eton. His younger brother Richard is seated to his right.

that he would echo in *The Spy Who Loved Me* when describing the early love life of his heroine Vivienne Michel. Only on the athletics field did he show any real application, becoming *Victor Ludorum*, or school sports champion. Fleming was so proud of this achievement that he referred to it, wryly, in the revealing jacket blurb for *Casino Royale*: 'Like his brother Peter – a more famous author – he was sent to Eton, where he was *Victor Ludorum* two years in succession, a distinction only once equalled – presumably by another second son trying to compensate for a brilliant older brother.'

In the premature obituary provided by M in *You Only Live Twice*, we learn that James Bond was expelled from Eton, after a 'brief and undistinguished' school career following 'some alleged trouble with one of the boys' maids', and was then sent to Fettes (the Eton equivalent in Scotland). Fleming escaped a similar fate when he was removed from Eton by his mother at the age of seventeen, a term early, sent to a tutorial crammer to prepare for the army entrance exams, and then duly crammed into the Royal Military Academy at Sandhurst, the training college for army officers.

By turns truculent and romantic, Fleming was not cut out for the regimented life of a Sandhurst cadet. His tutor, however, predicted that he would probably make a good soldier, 'provided always that the Ladies don't ruin him'. It was a prophetic remark. During one of his many forays outside the barracks, Fleming conceived a passion for Peggy Barnard, the attractive daughter of a colonel. On the evening of Sandhurst Sports Day, this blameless girl had agreed to attend an Oxford ball with another man, a date that so irritated Ian that he vowed, if she went ahead with it, to go to London and 'find myself a tart'. Peggy went to the ball, and Ian went to the Forty-Three Club in Soho, carried out his threat, and came down with a nasty dose of gonorrhoea. Fleming's enraged mother booked him into a nursing home, told the Sandhurst authorities that he was ill, and then pulled him out of the college altogether. In a last-ditch effort to instil some sort of balance in her increasingly wayward son (and if possible prepare him for the Foreign Office exams, her newest ambition for him), 'Mrs Val', as she was known, dispatched Ian to a finishing school, the Tennerhof, at Kitzbühel in the Austrian Alps.

The Tennerhof was a peculiar establishment, run by an eccentric English couple, Ernan and Phyllis Forbes Dennis, a former diplomat-spy and his novelist wife. Ian learned to ski, and spent much of his time conducting brief liaisons with the local girls. 'Technique in bed is important,' he wrote in a notebook, with somewhat unattractive languor. 'It is the scornful coupling that makes the affairs of Austrians and Anglo-Saxons so fragmentary and in the end so distasteful.' Far more important than brushing up his technique in bed and on the slopes, under the indulgent care of the Forbes Dennises, Fleming would begin to read, voraciously, and start to write, tentatively. Every evening, wild-haired Phyllis Forbes Dennis would spin fantastic stories at the dinner table (having spent the early part of each day in bed writing novels under a pseudonym), and she encouraged her pupils to do likewise. Many years later, Fleming would credit Phyllis with helping to launch his career as a writer, though it would take many more years for that talent to emerge. He wrote several poems and short stories, which were vivid and expressive if rather over-cooked.

In Fleming's memory, Kitzbühel was a 'golden time', and it was followed by two more years away from England, first in Munich and then Geneva. The young Englishman cut a dashing figure: he drove a smart black two-seater Buick, developed an excellent command of French and German, and enjoyed himself thoroughly. He also became engaged, briefly, to a young Swiss woman named Monique Panchaud de Bottomes, until his mother intervened. In 1931 he took the Foreign Office exams, but did not win a place. Young Fleming had successively failed to live up to expectations at Eton and Sandhurst, and now in his bid to join the Foreign Service.

At the age of twenty-one, Fleming was handsome in a somewhat vulpine way. A broken nose (acquired in a collision on the Eton football field with Henry Douglas-Home, brother of the future Prime Minister) added to his rakish allure. Here, then, was a man of athletic good looks and Scottish ancestry, dangerous to women, cultured and charming, with a taste for fast cars, expensive things and foreign adventures. His time at Eton had been an unmitigated failure, but he could ski beautifully, speak German fluently, and seduce effortlessly. Ernan Forbes Dennis said of his young pupil: 'He has excellent taste…and a desire both for truth and knowledge. He is virile and ambitious, generous and kind-hearted.' There was also something solitary and reserved about his character, a central hardness. All these things could be said of the young Fleming; in time, they would also be true of James Bond.

Mrs Val stepped in once more. Ian, she decreed, would become a journalist. Strings were pulled, and in October 1931 he took paid employment for the first time at Reuters news agency. This would prove a crucial formative experience. 'I learned to write fast, and above all, be accurate,' he recalled. 'In Reuters if you weren't accurate you were fired, and that was the end of that.' Accuracy, speed and

Monique Panchaud de Bottomes, the Swiss woman to whom Fleming became briefly engaged in 1931 while studying French and German at the University of Geneva.

OVERLEAF
Telegrams and newspapers relating to Fleming's trip to Moscow in 1939 to cover a trade mission to the USSR for *The Times*. Some believed Fleming's work was more closely related to espionage than journalism.

THE DUCE

PARIS DOUBTFUL

RESTRAINE
IN

BLEGRAM VIA NORTHERN

THE GREAT NORTHERN TELEGRAPH CO.
(LIMITED) of DENMARK.

Direct, speedy and reliable connection with CHINA, HONG KONG, JAPAN.
MACAO, MANILA, U.S.S.R., FINLAND, LATVIA, ESTONIA, LITHUANIA,
POLAND, SWEDEN, DENMARK, FAROE ISLANDS, ICELAND, and
GREENLAND.

D 480

*every night while Hudson is here*

3 16 04

15 23 1826

OSCOU YM27

PRESS = TIMES LDN

GMT NATIONAL
103 FLEMING

= PLEASE TELEPHONE EIGHT ROOM

HOTEL PHONE K 42500

*Call booked*

lease mark your cablegrams "VIA NORTHERN" and in order to avoid delay hand them in
ask us to collect them. Cablegrams are also accepted by Telephone London Wall 3636
messengers, etc., teleph... Doubtful words will b

AND TO ISSUE A
DEFENCE LOAN

SPONTANEOUS PUBLIC
CONTRIBUTIONS
FROM OUR OWN CORRESPONDENT

WARSAW, March 27

WORRIES

which has led the
in international affairs is
the difficulty of the economic
position. Allusions to it
both in the King's speech
of Signor Mussolini. The
first two months of the
published to-day, show
to ... 2,680,000,000
compared with
in the corresp...
ottling down of
Guarantee

The speech of Signor Mussolini is
generally regarded in Poland as marking
"no change on the Axis." Some
newspapers point out ... Some
may be regarded as ...
the democratic countries ...
lini's reaffirmation of ...
regarded as without ...
is argued that he ...
tactical political re...
turn to make a ...
from the Axis.
The official ... organ, Gazeta
emphasizes the "peaceful ...
speech, and ... regards ...
tion of the

LORD GORT
FRENCH A

Goebbels, the
left to-day for
days to Budapest and

W.F.C.
ROOM 1.
MR. BRAH

F.MoS
L.P.
H.S.
16

## FRANCO'S TWO OFFENSIVES

### FIGHTING SOUTH OF MADRID

### EMPT TO RALLY EPUBLICANS

r Special Correspondent

HEND 27 ...

their ment between Russia and the Unit ...

## TRADE WITH RUSSIA

### NEGOTIATIONS IN LONDON

### RESULTS OF MOSCOW TALKS

From Our Special Correspondent

MOSCOW, MARCH 27

Negotiations for a new Trade Agreement between Russia and the United King-
... standard at an early
... British Government that

## RUMANIAN TRADE AGREEMENT

### ASSURANCES FROM BUCHAREST

WESTMINSTER. MONDAY

MR. CHAMBERLAIN, answering a question
in the House of Commons to-day on the
German Agreement with Rumania, said
that its precise effect in practice would
depend on the manner in which its pro-
visions were carried out. In these circumstances the Government must await
developments before coming to any
definite conclusions.

The Rumanian Government, MR.
CHAMBERLAIN stated, had informed the
British Government that negotiations

## COT

### COOPE TH

### MR. STA

WES

All parties in
to-night were syn
industry in its a
giving a second re
to enable the indus
salvation. Th
the Bill will

*Russia
1939.*

PHONE MESSAGE    (Inward)

CORRESPONDENT    (Fleming)

EWS EDITOR

                                    March 27. 1939.

                    Received at 10pm by B.

I shall not be sending anything more from here. Warsaw
any future events.    I shall, however, still be here
address if you want to get into touch with me.
                    -----

                                            you

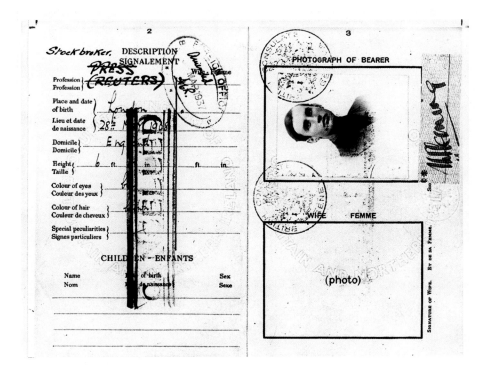

facts – the more colourful the better – these were the three key elements of a technique that would come to fruition with the Bond books. In addition, journalism would introduce Fleming to the wider world of international politics and foreign travel, the background for what was to come. In his first year in the job, Fleming covered the Alpine motor trials, an assignment that confirmed a growing fascination with fast cars, motor-racing and the associated high life, plus a Stalinist show trial of six British engineers accused of spying. Fleming's first taste of Moscow – gloomy, oppressive, granite-faced Communism – would inform his later images of Russian strength and menace. He loved it. With the chutzpah of youth, he formally requested an interview with Stalin; he was not surprised to be turned down, but was entirely astonished to received a note apparently signed by Stalin himself, explaining that he was simply too busy. The writer William Plomer, who met Fleming at this time, described him as 'like a mettlesome young horse' with 'a promise of something dashing and daring'. He seemed, thought Plomer, to 'smell some battle from afar'.

Having found a job he was good at, and enjoyed, Fleming promptly abandoned journalism for an exceptionally boring job in the City. The decision was perhaps less peculiar than it first seems. Robert Fleming had died, leaving nothing to his grandsons, whom he expected to be provided for by their father's estate. The nature of Val's will, however, meant that they would not inherit anything unless or until their mother remarried, or died. Such wills were not uncommon at the time, but it had a profound and unintended effect on Val's sons. The Fleming boys had been born to a world of money; the only problem was that they did not have very much of it. Ian Fleming, not for the last time in his life, decided to choose the more lucrative option and joined the merchant bank Cull & Co.

Fleming was not a good banker and soon shifted to stockbroking, to which he was even less suited. Indeed, one friend described him as 'the world's worst stockbroker'. His plan was simply to 'make a packet and then get out' – an ambition often stated by financial folk that seldom comes to pass, and even more rarely produces satisfaction. Fleming spent money as fast as he made it, on golf, cards, books (he would become an avid bibliophile) and women: young women from the cocktail party circuit, including a 'rather spiffing' nightclub dancer (or 'bubble girl') called Storm, but also older women – these older women were often intelligent, with strong personalities, and by no means naive poppets or stereotypical Bond Girls; they also tended to be married, usually to people Fleming knew. Whereas Bond goes to bed with a some quarters, unwelcome and unappreciated. The military attaché in Berlin dismissed Fleming's early intelligence-gathering efforts as 'gullible and of poor and imbalanced judgment'. Perhaps he had been actively recruited by British intelligence at some point in the 1930s, but if so, it seems likely that Fleming would have revealed as much in the end: like many people involved in espionage, he was not very good at keeping secrets. More probably, his well-connected mother told Montagu Norman, then Governor of the Bank of England, that her son was looking for an interesting war job, and Norman gave a nod to the right channels.

According to the old saw, anyone who asks to be a spy cannot be a spy. However it came about – whether through formal or informal contact, the old spy network, the old boy network or family clout – Ian Fleming was living proof that if you really wanted to join the espionage and intelligence club, you could. On 24 May 1939, just four months before the declaration of war, Fleming sat down to lunch at the Carlton Grill with Rear Admiral John Henry Godfrey, the hard-driving Director of Naval Intelligence (DNI) and the man responsible for gathering intelligence in all areas of the war related to British naval interests – in other words, just about everywhere. Godfrey, himself barely three months into the job, had put out the word that he needed an assistant. Fleming, he decided, would be the ideal candidate.

As, indeed, he was. To date, Fleming's combination of imagination, intelligence and charm had found no more useful outlet than half-hearted money-making and full-hearted self-indulgence. He would make a superb aide to the Director of Naval Intelligence: his ability to get on with most people, particularly older, self-important men, made him the perfect liaison between the irascible Godfrey and the other parts of the British intelligence machine; his as yet unrealised literary skills lent him the resourceful thinking and imagination that is essential to effective espionage; his gambler's instinct, his taste for adventure and his ability to read personality would all be honed and developed as the feckless bon viveur was transformed into Fleming of Naval Intelligence, a pivotal operative in Britain's secret war at sea. Much of Fleming's success was a consequence of his relationship with Godfrey: the admiral was M to Fleming's Bond – an uncompromising, precise, short-tempered and loyal older man, faced with a young, gifted and unorthodox assistant, to whom he granted extraordinary licence. Years later, Godfrey, noting Fleming's 'marked flair' for intelligence planning, would pay extravagant (and perhaps excessive) tribute to his protégé: 'Ian should have been DNI and I his naval adviser.' Reflecting

Fleming clad in his naval uniform in Room 39 of the Admiralty, the nerve centre of the Naval Intelligence Division. It was a smoky den crammed with desks, which one inhabitant likened to 'an Arab bank'.

years later on the inspiration for Bond, Fleming was precise: 'My job got me right to the heart of things.'

The Naval Intelligence Division (NID), operating out of Rooms 38 and 39 of the Admiralty, in Whitehall, was responsible for collecting, analysing and distributing intelligence for the Admiralty, and providing security and counter-intelligence to the Royal Navy for the war at sea. But its role was far wider than this suggests, just as Fleming was far more than merely an assistant to its boss. With two thousand personnel at its peak, and through a worldwide network of agents and attachés, NID assembled a vast amount of detailed information, but also formulated active deception plans and played an important part in the complex, fast-moving and dangerous game that is wartime espionage. In addition to signals intelligence and tracking U-boats and shipping, NID helped to run agents and double agents, and dealt in stolen documents, aerial photography, coastal surveillance and numerous 'special operations' against the Germans.

In the smoky hive of Room 39, Fleming was Godfrey's front man, and as such he operated with considerable freedom: he liaised with MI6 and SOE (responsible for sabotage and subversion); he worked with the Political Warfare Executive on propaganda, and handled the press; he fielded demands for information from above, and shielded Godfrey from interference from below. 'I shared all secrets with him,' Godfrey later wrote. Fleming was also allowed to evolve and manage his own plans, or 'plots', as he referred to them – the choice of word, given his later career as a novelist, seems significant. Some of Fleming's ideas were run-of-the-mill, some were fantastical and impractical, and some, in the opinion of his colleagues, were simply mad. Even Godfrey noted that Fleming tended not to let practicalities get in the way of a good 'plot': 'He had plenty of ideas and was anxious to carry them out but was not interested in, and would prefer to ignore, the extent of the logistics background inseparable to all projects.' In a sense, Fleming's task was to dream up espionage plans with convincing scenarios; others would then be charged with trying to turn fiction into reality. In this, he was preparing for, and precisely reversing, the process that would lead to the creation of James Bond.

Among Fleming's more remarkable ideas were: scuttling cement barges in the Danube at its most narrow point in order to block the waterway for German shipping; forging Reichsmarks to disrupt the German economy; dropping an observer (possibly Fleming himself) on the island of Heligoland to monitor the shipping outside Kiel; sinking a

The naval uniform worn by Pierce Brosnan in the 1997 film *Tomorrow Never Dies*.

lump of concrete off Dieppe with men inside it to observe the German coastal defences; luring German secret agents to Monte Carlo and capturing them; and floating a radio ship in the North Sea to broadcast depressing and/or irritating propaganda to the Germans. 'What nonsense they were,' Fleming would later write, 'those romantic Red Indian daydreams so many of us indulged in at the beginning of the war.' They may have seemed nonsensical in retrospect, but at the time they were matters of life and death, and Ian treated his new job with a dedication he had never shown before, starting work at 6 a.m. and continuing late into the night. 'It was deadly serious as well as intellectually stimulating,' wrote one colleague. Lieutenant Fleming received wartime promotions to acting lieutenant commander in the Royal Naval Volunteer Reserve, then acting commander – the same rank as James Bond.

'Operation Ruthless', which Fleming concocted in September 1940, offers an excellent example of his talents as both an espionage planner and a novelist. The cryptanalysts at Bletchley Park had already broken the code used on the fabled Enigma machine by the German Abwehr, or military intelligence service, but they had not yet penetrated

the mysteries of the code used by the German navy, which used a different coding machine. NID wanted a codebook, so Fleming came up with a plan. The Germans had begun operating a rescue boat in the English Channel to pick up downed pilots. If this boat, presumably carrying a codebook aboard, could be lured to pick up what looked like a downed German plane, the crew could be overpowered and the codebook seized. Fleming's plan came in three acts:

The Enigma coding machine, the German device used to encrypt and decrypt secret military messages. The breaking of the Enigma code was the greatest intelligence coup of the war.

Obtain from the Air Ministry an air-worthy German bomber. Pick a tough crew of five, including pilot, W/T (wireless/telegraph) officer and word-perfect German speaker. Dress them in German Air Force uniforms, add blood and bandages to suit.

Crash plane in the Channel after making SOS to rescue service.

Once aboard rescue boat, shoot German crew, dump overboard, bring rescue boat back to English port.

Fleming added a Bond touch, insisting that the pilot be a 'tough bachelor, able to swim'. A Heinkel He 111 bomber, shot down over Scotland and since repaired, was obtained, along with some German uniforms. The plan sounded simple, but, as with many Fleming plots, there were serious practical objections, not least the argument that a Heinkel crashed at speed might kill its crew on impact or sink so fast that all inside would drown. Undaunted, Ian proposed to accompany the crew in person, an idea that was flatly rejected by Godfrey: 'Ian was someone who simply could not fall into enemy hands because he was privy to everything.' To Fleming's chagrin, 'Operation Ruthless' was first postponed and then abandoned.

Despite such setbacks, Commander Fleming was not content to spend the war pushing paper from behind a desk, no matter how interesting the paper or how imposing the desk. In June 1940, Fleming apparently flew to Paris as France was collapsing under the German onslaught. There he is said to have extracted a large sum of money from the safe at the Rolls-Royce headquarters in Paris where MI6 kept its funds, before heading south to make contact with Admiral Jean-François Darlan, head of the French navy. Britain needed to know whether Darlan would come over to the British side, or whether his fleet might fall into German hands. Godfrey wanted Fleming to find out.

When Fleming arrived, Bordeaux was in chaos, teeming with refugees. The newly arrived naval lieutenant commander helped with

Fleming hints at Bond's heroic wartime service, recording that he saw action in the Ardennes forest in 1944, operated 'behind enemy lines', and killed two enemy agents during the war – a Japanese code-breaker at the Rockefeller Center in New York and a Norwegian double agent whom he stabs to death in Stockholm. Whether Ian Fleming would have liked to play a similarly dramatic part in the war is moot. John Godfrey was not about to allow him to head off to places where he might be killed: Fleming was simply too useful where he was, and, as 'the only officer who had a finger in practically every pie', he knew too much to risk being captured.

In the Bond novels, 007 is described as having spent much of the war travelling the world on various missions. That was certainly Fleming's lucky experience. Operation Golden Eye was the back-up plan to maintain communication with Gibraltar and launch sabotage operations in case the Nazis invaded Spain; setting up the plan, which never had to be used, took Fleming to Spain, Portugal, Tangiers and Gibraltar itself. It would also of course become the name of his Jamaican home. Fleming found himself in close contact with intelligence operatives in the United States, most notably the Canadian William Stephenson, head of British intelligence in North America, and William 'Big Bill' Donovan, the lawyer, First World War veteran and US government official who would play a crucial role in Anglo-American intelligence and the creation of the Office of Strategic Services (OSS), which would later evolve into the CIA.

In May 1941, Fleming accompanied Godfrey to the States, ostensibly to inspect security in US ports, but also to help William Stephenson and Donovan develop the intelligence relationship with America. On the way, they stopped at Estoril, near Lisbon, where Fleming gambled at the casino with some Portuguese businessmen, and lost. On leaving, Fleming remarked: 'What if those men had been German secret service agents, and suppose we had cleaned them out of their money; now that would have been exciting.' It was another glimpse into the workings of Fleming's imagination. The scene would marinade in his mind for a decade before finding its way into the most memorable moment in *Casino Royale*, when Bond cleans out the repulsive communist agent Le Chiffre.

In Washington, Godfrey and Fleming met J. Edgar Hoover, the head of the FBI, for exactly sixteen minutes, but soon afterwards Roosevelt followed British advice and made Bill Donovan head of the new government intelligence department that would later become the OSS. At Donovan's request, Fleming penned a seventy-page memo with suggestions on the shape a US intelligence agency should take

after the war. His description of the ideal secret agent has the unmistakable ring of Bond: 'must have trained powers of observation, analysis and evaluation; absolute discretion, sobriety, devotion to duty; language and wide experience, and be aged about 40 to 50'. Fleming would later claim, not entirely seriously, that this work had been instrumental in forming the CIA charter; even if this was not strictly true, Donovan was grateful enough to present Fleming with a .38 Colt revolver inscribed 'For Special Services'. In later life, Fleming would stoke speculation by declining to say exactly what these services had been, while hinting that they had been very special indeed.

Fleming made two more trips across the Atlantic, for conferences at which Churchill and Roosevelt discussed Allied strategy. The second, in Quebec in 1943, involved one of the odder moments in the Fleming–Bond biography. Bill Stephenson, the mastermind behind British intelligence in North America, would later claim that during this visit Fleming attended Camp X, the notoriously tough training centre near Toronto where SOE and OSS agents were put through their paces. More than that, Stephenson claimed that Fleming had excelled at the course, including unarmed combat, placing a fake bomb in a Toronto power station, swimming underwater to an offshore tanker and attaching a limpet mine to the hull (strongly reminiscent of a scene in *Live and Let Die*), and firing a Sten gun on the rifle range with 'extraordinary relish'. Most bizarrely, at the end of the course, each trainee was supposedly issued with a revolver and told to kill a man at a specific address. According to Stephenson, this was the only aspect of the course Fleming flunked; he would later declare that he 'could never kill a man in that way'.

However, the historian of Camp X, David Stafford, could find no evidence that Ian Fleming had ever attended a course there. The courses described by Stephenson, at which his friend supposedly excelled, were not on the curriculum. It is certainly possible, even likely, that he visited the camp in 1943; he may even have taken part in a few training events. But the notion that Fleming outperformed the real spies at the most demanding of all wartime spy camps is pure fiction, and soon would be.

Despite the sudden sacking of Admiral Godfrey in December 1942, as the war headed to its finale, Ian continued to play a prominent role in naval intelligence. His travels continued, including a round-the-world trip to coordinate intelligence for the new British Pacific Fleet that took him to Cairo, Ceylon, Australia and then home via Pearl Harbor. He also visited Jamaica to attend a conference on the U-boat threat in the Caribbean, and fell in love with the island. Here he would build his holiday home, Goldeneye, and here he would, in time, write every one of the Bond novels.

In March 1944, Fleming was charged with running the committee which channelled top-secret information to the Royal Navy units preparing to invade Normandy. The 'Red Indians', 30 AU, would be part of the attack, and Fleming compiled lists of the sort of information and equipment to be scooped up ahead of the invasion force. As the German army retreated, 30 AU scoured after it. Later, the unit would be the first Allied force to enter the naval port of Kiel. Fleming's 'Red Indians' picked up some astonishing technological booty: an acoustic homing torpedo hidden in a mushroom farm, an amphibious machine for exploding beach mines, and a one-man submarine – complete with decomposing crewman inside, one dead eye pressed to the periscope. At Tambach Castle, 30 AU came across the entire German naval archives dating back to 1870, under the care of three German admirals. Fleming

30 AU
COMMANDO UNIT
30 COMMANDO ASSAULT
THE F-S FIGHTING KNIFE
ATTAIN BY SURPRISE

The emblem of 30 AU, the 'Red Indians', the intelligence-gathering commando unit that Ian Fleming helped to create.

himself travelled to Germany to ensure their safe return to Britain. As for the three admirals, according to one account, Fleming ordered that they be killed, but when the lieutenant charged with this refused, he relented. Something about this story does not ring true: whatever brutal qualities he might invest in his fictional agent, Fleming was not the killing kind.

Fleming never claimed to be James Bond. He did not have to: the critics and media did that for him. But he was careful not to deny it too forcefully either. He was only too happy to be photographed with gun in hand, and to hint at dark doings in his wartime spy days. He had travelled the world helping to spin the wartime spy web, and he had seen fighting at first hand. However, most of his war had taken place behind a London desk, dreaming up plots; his second successful career would involve the same process, but at a different desk. In later years, Fleming would refer to 'school and war and other uncivilised experiences'; in truth, his war had been a remarkably civilised affair.

After six and a half years with naval intelligence, Fleming was no longer the callow, spoiled young man he had been in 1939. He had found a world, of secret agents and espionage, of adventure, violence and intrigue, that delighted him, satisfying both his intellect and romanticism. Churchill himself asserted that 'in the higher ranges of Secret Service work, the actual facts of many cases were in every respect equal to the most fantastic inventions of romance and melodrama. Tangle within tangle, plot and counter-plot, ruse and treachery, cross and double-cross, true agent, false agent, double agent, gold and steel, the bomb, the dagger and the firing party, were interwoven in many a texture so intricate as to be incredible and yet true.' Fleming would later quote that passage with approval, having converted his own experience of the tangled world into novels. It would be another seven years before he sat down to create Bond, but much of the material was already in place. Fleming had met dangerous adventurers, and known subtle spies; in the midst of war, he had travelled to distant corners of the world; he had witnessed the remarkable power of modern gadgetry in the spy's armoury; he had seen how secret agents are made; he had watched men die; and he had held the power of life and death in his own hands. Above all, his job with naval intelligence had taken place in a wartime world where anything seemed possible. Winning a war, like writing a novel, required one weapon above all others: imagination.

Back in London in 1946, Fleming returned to journalism and accepted the post of foreign news manager of the Kemsley newspaper group, which included the *Sunday Times*, the *Empire News*, the *Sunday Graphic* and a raft of local and regional newspapers. As the former press liaison officer for NID, he had struck up a close friendship with the proprietor, Lord Kemsley, during the war, and his contract was astonishingly generous: a fat wage for an undemanding job, a large expense account and, crucially, two months off in early spring of every year to spend in Jamaica. Fleming was manager of some eighty foreign correspondents, whose locations were indicated by a map behind his desk with a number of flashing lights. These correspondents (some of whom were also spies) were hired, fired, paid and commissioned by Fleming. Over the next fourteen years, he would perform numerous roles at the *Sunday Times*: manager, columnist and writer on subjects as diverse as gambling and travel. His was an easy, pleasant and unchallenging life. Fleming's description in *Moonraker* of Bond's daily routine when not on assignment is a fairly accurate depiction of his own easygoing existence in these years: 'Elastic office hours from around ten to six, lunch…evenings spent playing cards in the company of a few close friends…or making love, with rather cold passion, to

Ian Fleming (*foreground*) attends an editorial meeting at the *Sunday Times*, after accepting a job in 1946 as foreign news manager of the Kemsley newspaper group.

one of three similarly disposed married women, weekends playing golf for high stakes.'

But just as Bond secretly awaits the call from M, so Fleming was also preparing himself, perhaps subconsciously, for a belated call-up from his own muse: gathering material, honing his wartime memories, travelling the world, and preparing Bond's life within his own.

# 003

## WHO WAS JAMES BOND?

Every acquaintance of Ian Fleming ran the risk of ending up as a character, or a characteristic, in one of his Bond books. Fleming was, like most fiction writers, an avid collector of facts: he gathered names, plots, meals, venues and words from the places he had been and the people he had met. Reality underpins the fiction: while producing the stream of Bond books, Fleming would also find time to write two books of non-fiction, on diamonds and travel, both subjects which loom large in the novels. Almost every character in his fiction is based, to some extent, on a real person, even if only by name. He plucked these names from his social circle, his memory, his reading, his favourite Jamaican newspaper, the *Daily Gleaner*, and his imagination: old school friends (and enemies), clubmen, colleagues in the City and Fleet Street, golfing partners, girlfriends and others found themselves transported into Fleming's fiction. This was all very well if you happened to be named after a heroic bit-part player or a curvaceous new lover, but several of Fleming's acquaintances were mortally offended to discover that their names had been appropriated and attached to the most fearsome fictional villains. The Bond books are not *romans-à-clef*, straightforward fictionalisations of living people, but rather careful, teasing and often witty interleavings of fact and fiction, imagined people with real names, and real people with invented names in imagined situations. Working out who's who in Bond, and who might be partially based on whom (as well as who later claimed to be whom, and probably wasn't), is one of the most intriguing and complex aspects of the relationship between Ian Fleming and James Bond.

Where did James Bond – the name – come from? As with all aspects of the Bond stories, there are several theories and a number of speculations. The most popular (and one that he publicly affirmed) is that Fleming, sitting down to work at his desk in Goldeneye, simply lifted the name from his bookshelves, his eye having alighted upon *Field Guide to Birds of the West Indies* by James Bond, the standard reference book published by Macmillan in 1947. Fleming was fascinated

Norman Parkinson's portrait of Ian Fleming in suitably James Bond-like pose. Fleming disliked shooting and knew little about guns, avoiding them whenever possible.

by wildlife, and birds in particular: 'For Your Eyes Only' opens with a detailed description of the streamer-tail or doctor hummingbird, which again may be derived from the other James Bond. In 1964, long after his name had become a global brand, the American ornithologist paid a surprise visit to Fleming in Jamaica. A Canadian film crew happened to be conducting an interview with Fleming at the time, and with a happy flourish, the author introduced his unexpected guest as 'the real James Bond'. In the film *Die Another Day*, starring Pierce Brosnan, Bond picks up a copy of *Field Guide to Birds of the West Indies* and disguises himself as an ornithologist, in elaborate homage to the origin of the name.

Though James Bond may have been christened after an expert bird-spotter plucked at random from a book spine, it is possible that the name was already stored somewhere in Fleming's mind when he began to write *Casino Royale*. During the war, C. H. Forster, a friend who was then working in the Ministry of Aircraft Production, recalled a casual conversation in which Fleming described how he planned to come up with fictional names if he wrote a book. 'That's easy,' he said. 'I think of the first couple of names in my house at school and change their Christian names.' Forster told him that the first names in *his* school register had been James Aitken and Harry Bond. 'So you could have Harry Aitken and James Bond'. Fleming had allegedly remarked that 'James Bond' sounded better. There are other possibilities. Peter Fleming knew an SIS officer named Rodney Bond, who had saved his life during a clandestine operation in Greece. According to the British diplomat Harold Caccia (who had been rescued by Rodney Bond in the same operation), when Ian Fleming was looking for a name for his fictional hero, it was his brother Peter who suggested he be named in honour of his wartime colleague. There is also a character named James Bond in the Agatha Christie short story 'The Rajah's Emerald', published in 1934: Fleming may have read the story, leaving the name lodged somewhere in his subconscious. Bondologists have also noted that there is a church in Toronto called St James Bond, which Fleming might conceivably have seen on his visit to Canada during the war – although his Bond, of course, is no kind of saint.

Any, all or none of these factors may have contributed to the naming of Bond. What is certain is that once he had alighted on the name, Fleming knew it fitted his spy like a Savile Row suit. 'I wanted the simplest, dullest, plainest-sounding name I could find,' he said, something 'brief, unromantic, Anglo-Saxon and yet very masculine.' A name like 'Peregrine Maltravers', he reflected, would be too exotic for a man intended to be a 'neutral figure – an anonymous blunt instrument wielded by a Government Department'. What Fleming did not say is that 'Peregrine Maltravers' is also an avowedly *upper-class* English name. Scottish-born Bond, for all his clubbable ways and public school education, is intended to be classless (or as classless as an upper-class man like Fleming could make him). The bi-syllabic James Bond has a double-barrelled simplicity to it. 'Bond' sounds oddly British and reassuring: a bond is what an Englishman's word is made of, the financial security one may reliably invest in, the adhesive that holds things together. With no offence to Peregrines worldwide, this is not a name women tend to go to bed with on first acquaintance, and the phrase 'The name's Maltravers, Peregrine Maltravers' hardly trips off the tongue. In *The Man with the Golden Gun*, Bond, refusing a knighthood, reflects on his own name: 'No middle name. No hyphen. A quiet, dull, anonymous name.'

The codename 007 may have a simpler origin. One of the greatest triumphs of British naval intelligence in the First World War had been the breaking of the code in the fabled Zimmermann Telegram of 1917, which helped bring the United States into the war and effectively sealed Germany's defeat. The telegram, sent by German Foreign Minister Arthur Zimmermann, instructed the German ambassador in Mexico to approach the Mexican government with a view to forming an alliance against the US. The message was intercepted and decoded by three naval intelligence code-breakers, working out of Room 40 in the Admiralty; two months later, an outraged US Congress declared war on Germany. The German diplomatic code used in the top-secret telegram was identified by the number 0075; thereafter the double-zero code was attached to all highly classified documents. To anyone versed in intelligence history, 007 signified the highest achievement of British military espionage. 'When I was in the Admiralty during the war,' Fleming told a later interviewer, 'all the top-secret signals had the double-O prefix. Although this was later changed for security reasons, it stuck in my mind and I decided to borrow it for Bond to make his job more interesting and provide him with a licence to kill.' The sixteenth-century English mathematician, occultist and secret agent, Dr John Dee, used a similar code in messages sent to Queen Elizabeth I. In Dee's code the double-O prefix, symbolising two eyes, was shorthand for 'For Your Eyes Only'.

Like most fictional characters, James Bond is not one individual. 'He was a compound of all the secret agents and commando types I met during the war,' Fleming once declared. 'It was all the things that I heard and learned about secret operations that finally led me to write about them in a disguised way and with James Bond as the

central character.' Fleming never denied that Bond was a combination of real people; he did not, however, identify exactly *which* people, leaving the door open to an entire raft of claimants. Fleming compounded the issue by flattering more than one person with the suggestion that he was the model for the super-spy; inevitably, as Bond's fame spread, this was an increasingly coveted accolade.

Chief among the contenders is, of course, Fleming himself. The physical descriptions of 007 recall his creator, with his 'longish nose' and slightly 'cruel mouth'. They even share the same colour (blue) eyes and black hair. In *From Russia with Love*, Fleming provides the most detailed picture of Bond, complete with elements of self-portraiture: 'The eyes wide and level under straight, rather long black eyebrows…the line of the jaws rather straight but firm.' In *Casino Royale*, Bond's looks remind the doomed beauty Vesper Lynd of Hoagy Carmichael, the American songwriter, singer and actor. The comparison is made again in *Moonraker*, in which Bond is described as 'certainly good-looking… Rather like Hoagy Carmichael in a way. That black hair falling down over the right eyebrow. Much the same bones. But there was something a bit cruel in the mouth, and the eyes were cold.' An image of Bond, approved by Fleming as part of the *Daily Express* strip cartoon that started in 1958, makes 007 appear faintly vampiric, but again bears more than a passing resemblance to Fleming himself. Fleming sometimes played up the autobiographical aspects of Bond, and sometimes downplayed them: 'I couldn't possibly be James Bond,' he told his friend, William Plomer. 'He's got more guts than I have. He's also considerably more handsome.'

Val Fleming, the courageous father killed in the trenches of the First World War, must have a primary claim to be the inspiration for James Bond. The father, dead when Ian Fleming was just eight years old, naturally left a permanent hole in Fleming's world, which Bond may partly have filled by representing his ideal man of action. It is possible, though simplistic, to see Bond as an expression of father/hero-worship played out in fiction, though Val was far too fastidious, gentle and conventional to be confused with the hard-eyed Bond.

Peter Fleming, Ian's much-admired elder brother, may have come a little closer to that model, being handsome, tough and, most importantly, a secret warrior. Having forged one career in peacetime as a highly successful travel writer, Peter had enjoyed an adventurous war. Drafted early into the world of military intelligence and irregular warfare, he was sent to Norway on a reconnaissance mission to plot a counter-attack following the Nazi invasion, and was erroneously reported killed. Mirroring Ian's role in naval intelligence, Peter had become assistant to the chief of military intelligence, and thus privy to some of the most delicate and fascinating secrets of wartime spying. He again narrowly escaped death while on an SOE mission to Greece, and was then transferred to Delhi, where he spent three years organising deception plans quite as elaborate as anything dreamed up by his brother. One such plot involved planting a briefcase full of forged papers in a crashed jeep in the jungle, to try to convince the advancing Japanese that they were facing an unexpectedly strong British force. After the war, Peter returned to writing and produced a novel, *The Sixth Column*, which had as its main character a thriller writer who creates a protagonist with marked similarities to Bond. In at least three ways, then, Peter helped to create Bond: by a successful writing career that may initially have put off his younger brother but later spurred him on to try his hand at fiction; by a wartime intelligence career with some enviably Bond-like aspects; and by writing a book that uncannily prefigured Ian's own literary career. Just six months after Peter published *The Sixth Column*, Ian set to work on *Casino Royale*.

Behind the Flemings follow a parade of swashbuckling types, each with a claim to a little of the Bond myth. One of the earliest is Conrad O'Brien-Ffrench, the skiing spy Fleming had first met in Kitzbühel back in the 1930s, when the older man was gathering information on German troop deployments as part of the Z Organisation, an amateur spy network made up of journalists and businessmen. While Fleming certainly met and admired this extraordinary character, he is unlikely to have known about his espionage activities in enough detail to use them as material in the Bond series.

A more likely candidate is Patrick Dalzel-Job, who served in the 30 AU unit during the latter part of the war. Dalzel-Job displayed many of Bond's characteristics: he was a superb marksman who had learned how to ski backwards, parachute behind enemy lines, dive, and pilot a miniature submarine. When on assignment, he wore an airman's jacket with a compass hidden inside one of the buttons and carried a pipe with a hidden chamber containing maps. Jan Aylen, technical officer with 30 AU, declared Dalzel-Job to be 'one of the most enterprising, plucky and resourceful' warriors he had ever met. Like Fleming, Dalzel-Job had lost his father in the trenches, and spent much of his youth navigating around the Norwegian coast with his mother, gaining a specialist knowledge that proved invaluable when war was declared and he signed up with British Naval Intelligence. Serving with the North Western Expeditionary Force in Norway in 1940, Dalzel-Job revealed a Bond-like streak of rebellion when he

Patrick Dalzel-Job, the naval intelligence officer and commando whose extraordinary exploits during the Second World War brought him into contact with Ian Fleming. Dalzel-Job was one of the principal inspirations for the character of 007.

disobeyed a direct order and insisted on evacuating five thousand Norwegian civilians from the town of Narvik who were facing imminent Nazi retaliation. He escaped a court martial after King Haakon of Norway awarded him the Knight's Cross of St Olav in recognition of his gallantry, 'making it difficult for me to be disciplined', in his own words.

By the time Fleming met him in 1944, Dalzel-Job had already won a reputation for bravery just this side of lunacy, which continued to expand in the closing months of the war. Striking out from Utah Beach after the D-Day landings with a handful of Royal Marines, he filleted vital intelligence from an abandoned flying-bomb site, disabled a German destroyer and personally accepted the surrender of the German city of Bremen. He then immediately set off on a quixotic quest to find the Norwegian woman who had once served as crew on his boat, and married her three weeks later.

Throughout his long life, Dalzel-Job, who died in 2003 at the age of ninety, was credited with being the model for James Bond. He never denied the association, and claimed that Fleming had told him, long after the war, that he was indeed an inspiration for Bond. But disarmingly, this diminutive figure with large ears who lived in retirement in the Scottish Highlands pointed out that in certain respects he was no Bond: 'I have never read a Bond book or seen a Bond movie. They are not my style… And I only ever loved one woman, and I'm not a drinking man.' Yet he also implied that he knew what was in the books and films, and recognised himself. 'When you have lived such an exciting life you don't need to see a fictional account of it,' he said, adding, perhaps unnecessarily, since he was approaching the age of eighty-seven: 'I prefer the quiet life now.' It is possible that the villain Oddjob in *Goldfinger* may be a sly joke on the name Dalzel-Job.

Dalzel-Job may have the strongest claim to be Bond, but he was not the only prototype among the ranks of hard men in naval special operations. Another was Michael Mason, the scion of a landed Oxfordshire family who ran away to become a fur-trapper in rural Canada and then enjoyed a second career as a successful amateur boxer. At the outbreak of war, the rugged Mason was operating as an agent in Romania when two Nazi agents were sent to assassinate him; he killed them both. Another with a claim to a bit of Bond was the extraordinary Merlin Minshall, an amateur racing driver who took part in Fleming's abortive attempt to disrupt traffic on the Danube by scuttling six cement barges at the river's narrowest point, the Iron Gates. Minshall, who had spent much of his life sailing the waterways of Europe, simply walked into Room 39 in 1939 and suggested the idea

off his own bat. Minshall was sent to Bucharest in 1940 with orders to
help Mason carry out the scheme. The cement barges were duly chartered
and headed up the Danube to the Iron Gates, with Minshall following
behind in a high-speed launch. Everything went wrong: the launch ran out
of fuel, the plan was betrayed and the local Nazis appeared. In true Bond
tradition, Minshall then set off in the launch and escaped, it is said, after
a two-hour high-speed chase. Minshall, who spent the latter part of
the war tracking U-boats and worked as naval liaison to Tito's partisans
in Yugoslavia, was one of the first to claim consanguinity with Bond.

A similar man of action was Fitzroy Maclean, the diplomat,
writer and adventurer who carried out covert operations behind the
lines in North Africa as part of the newly formed SAS, and later played
a pivotal role liaising with Tito's partisans in Yugoslavia. In 1942, he
abducted at gunpoint a Nazi sympathiser in Persia, General Zahidi, and
spirited him out of the country. Fleming first met Maclean in Moscow
in 1939, when he was on special assignment for *The Times*. Maclean,
then serving as a junior diplomat at the Moscow embassy, was sent
to summon Fleming to a dinner and found him in flagrante delicto in
his hotel room with an attractive Russian woman (who turned out to
be a Soviet plant, sent to spy on the journalist). Maclean told the dinner

party hostess that Fleming could not attend as he was 'very, very busy'. Despite their shared interests, the friendship between the two men appears to have cooled after the war. Fleming later considered Maclean's superb book *Eastern Approaches* for serialisation in the *Sunday Times*, then rejected it rather pointedly, insisting that the author had claimed too much credit for himself – something Fleming would surely not have done had Maclean been the inspiration for Bond.

The playboy double agent Dušan 'Duško' Popov, codenamed 'Tricycle' by the British, is yet another individual cited as a proto-Bond: certainly he shared many of Bond's (and for that matter Fleming's) tastes, including casinos, women, fast cars, expensive clothes and strong drink. Throughout the war, in the guise of an international businessman, Popov fed MI5-supplied disinformation to the German Abwehr, which continued to regard (and pay) him as one of its best spies. Fleming may well have known of Tricycle's exploits, but it is highly unlikely that they ever met. In one celebrated incident, Popov was gambling in Lisbon when he became irritated by the attitude of a large and vulgar Lithuanian, who kept showing off by calling '*Banque ouverte!*' whenever he held the bank, to indicate there was no upper limit on the stakes. Popov slapped $30,000 on the table – money which belonged to MI5. The Lithuanian, eyes bulging, declined the bet. Having successfully called his bluff, Popov tucked the money back in his dinner jacket and walked out. The incident became part of the Popov legend, and may have formed part of the inspiration for the gambling scenes in *Casino Royale*. Louche, charming and insufferably vain, Popov was a nerveless secret agent who, like Bond, never hesitated in his duty and seemed to care not one whit for the victims and wronged women he left in his wake. In later life, when asked whether he was an inspiration for James Bond, Popov managed to imply that he was more Bond than Bond himself. In 1981, he told a group of Italian journalists: 'I doubt whether a flesh and blood Bond would last forty-eight hours as a spy.'

In a similar mould was Wilfred 'Biffy' Dunderdale, the station chief of SIS (MI6) in Paris, whom Fleming met in 1940. A regular at Maxim's restaurant on the rue Royale, exquisite in Cartier cufflinks and handmade suit, and driving an armour-plated Rolls-Royce through Paris, the fashionable multilingual Dunderdale had much of Bond's style. He was also a most effective spy, having played a key role in the intelligence work that led to the cracking of the Enigma code – arguably the greatest coup in espionage history.

No account of possible Bond prototypes would be complete without mentioning William Stephenson, the Canadian spy chief

Wilfred 'Biffy' Dunderdale, the debonair station chief of MI6 in Paris, whose contacts with French and Polish intelligence helped to secure a model of the Enigma machine and break the German code.

Wilfred 'Biffy' Dunderdale, the debonair station chief of MI6 in Paris, whose contacts with French and Polish intelligence helped to secure a model of the Enigma machine and break the German code.

codenamed 'Intrepid', who ran British intelligence in North America. We know that Fleming and Stephenson were friends and allies. Stephenson boosted the legend of Fleming as Bond, and the writer returned the compliment. In a letter to the *Sunday Times* in October 1962, Fleming declared: 'James Bond is a highly romanticised version of a true spy. The real thing is…William Stephenson.' This has been taken to imply that the 'quiet Canadian' was the main inspiration for Bond, which is not exactly what Fleming was saying. Stephenson was, indeed, 'the real thing'; he was, in Fleming's own assessment, 'very tough, very rich, single-minded, patriotic and a man of few words'. He had had an extraordinary career in the First World War, during which he was gassed, learned to fly with the Royal Flying Corps, shot down Lothar von Richthofen, brother of the celebrated Red Baron, crashed, was captured and escaped. But by the second war he was middle-aged, and no longer the type to be indulging in car chases and love affairs. Working without a salary, under the official title of British Passport Control Officer, Stephenson used the so-called British Security Coordination (a front for British intelligence) to influence American opinion, channel top-secret information, and train secret agents at Camp X in Ontario. Some two thousand agents would pass through this camp during the course of the war, five of whom would go on to direct the CIA. Stephenson's plan (which never materialised) to obtain nearly three million dollars in gold belonging to the Vichy government from the Caribbean island of Martinique, may have inspired the plot of *Goldfinger*, in which the arch-villain seeks to empty Fort Knox. Stephenson's plot involved overthrowing the Vichy authorities on the island, getting the colony to declare for General de Gaulle, and then handing the gold reserves over to the Free French. Stephenson undoubtedly played a vital role in Britain's wartime espionage and taught Fleming much of the craft he knew so well, but in many ways he is closer to M, the veteran spymaster, than to Bond himself.

There is no definitive answer to the question, who was 'the real Bond', since, as he is a fictional creation, there was no such thing. Teasing apart the claims and counterclaims is made harder by the fact that spies lie so easily, particularly when remembering their own lives. The entertaining memoirs of Popov, Minshall and Stephenson should all be taken with large quantities of salt. Bond is all of the above, and none of them: he possesses the cunning of William Stephenson, the sheer toughness of Michael Mason, the insouciant style of Popov, the disobedience of Dalzel-Job, the elegant cufflinks of Biffy Dunderdale, the courage of Merlin Minshall, and Fitzroy Maclean's intelligent heroism. Bond is all of these, but flavoured throughout with a healthy dollop of Fleming himself and his remarkable family. These intoxicating elements were then shaken up together, and stirred.

Bernard Lee in the role of 'M', James Bond's irascible and indulgent boss. In *The Man with the Golden Gun*, Fleming finally reveals his name: Vice Admiral Sir Miles Messervy, KCMG.

## Who was M?

At first this seems a far easier question to answer, but, as with all Fleming stories, the plot is thicker than it seems. The fictional Admiral Sir Miles Messervy KCMG (finally identified by name in *The Man with the Golden Gun*) is based, in large part, on John Godfrey, Fleming's boss at the Naval Intelligence Department. M is grumpy, dedicated, rude and every inch the naval martinet, with 'damnably clear' bright blue eyes; his underlings are terrified and loyal in equal parts. He 'thinks in the language of battleships', and his voice is straight off the Quarterdeck (the name of his house). Kingsley Amis assiduously totted up the various ways M's voice is described by Fleming: angry (3); brutal, cold (7); curt, dry (5); gruff (7); stern, testy (5); and so on. Yet this is the voice Bond 'loved and obeyed'. All these traits were apparent in Godfrey, who nonetheless ran a tight ship and proved a most effective spymaster. Fleming described him as a 'real war-winner' with 'the mind and

character of a Bohemian mathematician'. Some found Godfrey impossible to deal with, and his abrupt sacking in 1942 (and lack of wartime decoration) has never been fully explained. But, like Bond, Fleming knew how to play his short-tempered boss, and was treated with similar indulgence: M lets Bond get away with, and periodically commissions him for, murder. In *On Her Majesty's Secret Service*, Fleming makes the M–Godfrey link most explicit, describing the door-knocker on M's house as the ship's bell clapper from 'HMS *Repulse*', which 'had been M's final sea-going appointment'. Godfrey's last command, before taking over at NID, had been the *Repulse*.

Rear Admiral John Godfrey, Fleming's boss as Director of Naval Intelligence, and the principal model for 'M'. Grumpy and demanding, Godfrey was nonetheless 'a real war winner', in Fleming's estimation.

In a strange case of truth following fiction, Godfrey would eventually ask Fleming to write his biography (Fleming declined), yet it seems the inspiration for M was not entirely pleased to be immortalised as the boss of a cold-blooded killer, who was prepared to employ Bond to kill the crooks who had murdered his friends (in 'For Your Eyes Only'). 'He turned me into that unsavoury character, M,' Godfrey complained after Fleming's death. 'Ian wanted people to take M seriously and questioned me closely about his notional age and career. The end result did not convince or thrill.'

The use of the single initial was a convention dating back to Mansfield Cumming-Smith, the first head of SIS (MI6), who became known as 'C' after his habit of initialling papers he had read with a C written in green ink. In Somerset Maugham's *Ashenden* stories, another source of inspiration for Fleming, the same post is occupied by 'R', the grim, amoral spy chief who is prepared to expend his agents ruthlessly without ever dirtying his own hands. Alongside the fictional R and the real C, there are three more Ms and one Z, all real, all known to Fleming, and all parts of the composite character that emerged as M.

'Colonel Z', Lieutenant Colonel Sir Claude Dansey, was Deputy Chief of SIS and head of the shadowy Z network of which Conrad O'Brien-Ffrench was a part. The bespectacled Dansey was witty, spiteful, charming and slightly mad. As a boy of sixteen, Dansey, who was not homosexual, was seduced by Oscar Wilde. His father threatened to prosecute, and then packed the young Claude off to Africa. He was first recruited as a spy during the Boer War, lost his money in the Wall Street Crash, performed various duties for British intelligence before the Second World War, and then abruptly quit, allowing rumours to circulate that he had been sacked for stealing. Meanwhile, believing SIS to be ill-organised and inefficient, he set about building a parallel organisation behind the cover of a respectable import–export business in Bush House, recruiting part-time, usually unpaid agents, including journalists, businessmen, gamblers and playboys. Dansey's agents used the codename Z, and avoided using the wireless for messages. In 1939, the Z network was absorbed into SIS, and as assistant to the new 'C', Stewart Menzies, Dansey helped to coordinate active espionage until the end of the war. Fleming gives him a namecheck in *From Russia with Love*, when Darko Kerim, Bond's friend who is murdered on the *Orient Express*, refers to 'Major Dansey', his predecessor as Head of Section T. Two famous men who worked in wartime intelligence with the real Dansey gave very different assessments of Colonel Z: Malcolm Muggeridge called him 'the only professional in MI6'; the historian Hugh Trevor-Roper, Lord Dacre, however, considered him 'an utter shit, corrupt, incompetent, but with a certain low cunning'.

Major-General Sir Colin McVean Gubbins was director of operations and training with SOE, and the creator of the auxiliary units on which Peter Fleming worked, intended to operate behind the lines in Britain in the event of a German invasion. An expert in guerrilla warfare, he was described by the cryptographer Leo Marks as 'a real Highland toughie, bloody brilliant...with a moustache which was as clipped as his delivery and eyes which didn't mirror his soul or any other such trivia. The general's eyes reflected the crossed swords on his shoulders, warning all comers not to cross them with him.' Since the initial C was already taken, and G is an initial commonly used as an army abbreviation, Gubbins signed himself by his middle initial: M.

Another contender is the equally strange MI5 spymaster Maxwell Knight, who ran a subsection of the security service responsible for rooting out potential extremist subversives in Britain, both fascist and communist. Knight broke up some of the most important spy rings in Britain, and was one of the first to warn that the secret services were being infiltrated by communist moles, but his warnings were fatally ignored. Knight was a man of many parts, most of them very odd and quite incompatible: in addition to running a huge and elaborate spy ring, he was a novelist, a jazz saxophonist who had been taught by the great Sidney Bechet, and an occultist who befriended and recruited the bizarre black magician Aleister Crowley. He was also an obsessive and inspired naturalist who kept snakes in the bath and wrote such definitive works as *How to Keep a Gorilla*. Ostensibly, Knight was a ladies' man: he was married three times (and briefly suspected of murdering one of his wives), filled his office with beautiful young women, ran two of the most successful female agents in British wartime history, and wrote a peculiar guide to running women agents, which includes a section on using sex as bait, in so-called honey traps. 'It is difficult to imagine

Maxwell Knight, the wartime MI5 agent-runner who signed his memos 'M', and who ended his life as a much-loved presenter of nature programmes on the BBC.

To Katie
With affection from
Father
April 1906

J.F.Langhans

anything more terrifying than for an officer to become landed with a woman-agent who suffers from an overdose of Sex,' he wrote. This slightly odd statement may perhaps be explained by the fact that Knight never consummated any of his marriages, and was probably homosexual. Maxwell Knight signed all his memos 'M', and was certainly well known to Fleming, although they never worked together. After the war, Knight would move effortlessly from a career in spying to a new career as a naturalist, ending his life as a much-loved BBC presenter of nature programmes.

There is one last real-life 'M', who may have helped to form the fictional M. William Melville, an Irish-born policeman who died in the last year of the First World War, has a good claim to be Britain's first secret service chief. Born in Kerry, Melville made his name foiling Fenian and anarchist bomb plots in Britain, and inspired the character of the detective in Joseph Conrad's *The Secret Agent*. Melville recruited Sidney Reilly, the so-called 'Ace of Spies', learned the art of lock-picking from Harry Houdini, and foiled the 1887 Golden Jubilee Plot to assassinate Queen Victoria. On his 'retirement' from the police in 1903, Melville founded a secret service, the forerunner of MI5, and adopted the codename 'M'. Using the pseudonym William Morgan, he gathered intelligence for the War Office, and when the Secret Service Bureau was established in 1909 to coordinate both home and foreign intelligence (later MI5 and MI6), Melville was recruited as chief detective. Fleming would certainly have been aware of the exploits of this other 'M', which had become a part of intelligence legend by the time he arrived at NID.

There is one final intriguing hypothesis, advanced by John Pearson, Fleming's biographer, to the effect that M might conceivably be modelled on Eve Fleming. Certainly, 'M' was Ian's nickname for his mother from early childhood. She, like M, was by turns strict and indulgent, loved and feared. As Pearson writes, 'While Fleming was young, his mother was certainly one of the few people he was frightened of, and her sternness toward him, her unexplained demands, and her remorseless insistence on success find a curious and constant echo in the way M handles that hard-ridden, hard-killing agent, 007.'

William Melville, the Irish-born policeman who founded a secret service that would evolve into MI5, and who used the codename 'M'.

## Who was Miss Moneypenny?

M's comely, love-struck secretary, the loyal keeper of secrets, has almost as many potential real lives as she has had appearances on screen. Miss Moneypenny's role in the books is comparatively small and, apart from her being a non-smoking, milk-drinking poodle-owner, we know little of her life. She 'would have been desirable but for eyes which were cool and direct and quizzical'. In *Thunderball* we learn that she 'often dreamed hopelessly about Bond'. Miss Moneypenny's yearning is made much more explicit in the films, and became a staple of the genre, the longest flirtation in film history, a central element in the badinage that precedes every Bond mission. Her amorous life is unfulfilled, but her career prospers, at least in the popular culture, as 'Britain's last line of defence'. By the time *You Only Live Twice* was filmed, she had been promoted to the rank of second officer in the Wrens, the Women's Royal Naval Service.

Lois Maxwell played the role of Miss Moneypenny, 'Britain's last line of defence', in the first fourteen James Bond films.

In the books Bond has his own secretary, Loelia Ponsonby, shared with 008 and 0011. The real Loelia Ponsonby was a friend of the Flemings who would become the Duchess of Westminster. When her marriage broke down, 'Lil' Ponsonby is said to have fallen for Ian himself, describing him as 'the most attractive man I've ever met'. For his part, Fleming described the fictional Loelia Ponsonby as 'tall and dark, with a reserved unbroken beauty', but added, 'unless she married soon, Bond thought for the hundredth time, or had a lover, her cool air of authority might easily become spinsterish' – which probably did not please the real 'Lil' one bit. It is possible that the duchess objected to seeing her real name hijacked for the purposes of popular literature. This may explain why, in *On Her Majesty's Secret Service*, Ponsonby abruptly retires after marrying a member of the Baltic Exchange ship-broking company, and is replaced as Bond's secretary by Mary Goodnight – a name with echoes of Fleming's own secretary at the *Sunday Times*, Una Trueblood (a name he would appropriate for the secretary murdered in *Dr No*). Both of Bond's secretaries are slight characters compared to Moneypenny, whose film persona is now almost as famous as Bond himself.

The name Moneypenny is derived from a character in an unfinished novel written by Peter Fleming after the war, entitled *The Sett*. The novel came to a halt after about thirty thousand words, but Miss Moneypenny survived in Ian's memory. The principal model for the Moneypenny character appears to have been a Miss Kathleen Pettigrew, who was the personal assistant to Stewart Menzies, Director General of MI6. In the first draft of *Casino Royale*, M's secretary was

'Miss Pettavel', or 'Petty', but Fleming clearly felt that was too close to reality and changed it. Miss Pettigrew was something of a legend in espionage circles: anyone attempting to gain access to 'C', as Fleming must have done, had first to pass through his terrifying secretary, who was brisk, intensely efficient and not remotely seductive. One former colleague described her as a 'formidable, grey-haired lady with the square jaw of the battleship type'.

Another strong possibility is Victoire 'Paddy' Bennett, who worked as a secretary in Room 39 and knew Fleming well. Bennett worked on 'Operation Mincemeat', the successful deception plan which involved planting a corpse with fake papers on the coast of Spain to persuade the Nazis that the Allies would attack Greece and Sardinia rather than Sicily. Ewen Montagu of NID was an architect of this ruse, and Fleming would probably have been at least tangentially involved. Paddy Bennett once described her former colleague, somewhat tartly, as 'definitely James Bond, in his mind'. She went on to marry Sir Julian Ridsdale, the long-serving MP for Harwich, and was made a Dame of the British Empire for her work with the Parliamentary Wives Club – a role that has a distinctly Moneypennyish ring to it.

Vera Atkins, executive officer with 'F' (French) Section, SOE, was described in her *New York Times* obituary in 2000 as 'widely believed to have inspired the character of Miss Moneypenny'. The unmarried Atkins was discreet, handsome and probably known to Fleming through his liaison duties. Though recruited as a secretary, Atkins swiftly emerged as a remarkable intelligence officer in her own right, briefing and dispatching more than five hundred SOE agents to occupied France; after the war she spent years trying to ascertain their fates.

In the end, Moneypenny was surely more fantasy than reality, not least because of the way Bond speaks to her. In *Thunderball*, when Moneypenny teases him about having to go to a health farm, he warns her: 'Any more ticking off from you and when I get out of this place I'll give you such a spanking you'll have to do your typing off a block of Dunlopillo.' Miss Moneypenny has an instant comeback: 'I don't think you'll be able to do much spanking after living on nuts and lemon juice for two weeks, James.' It is hard to imagine Fleming having such a conversation with any of the no-nonsense women he knew from wartime intelligence, let alone carrying out his spanking threat.

Vera Atkins, executive officer with the French section of the Special Operations Executive (SOE), and a brilliant intelligence professional who spent many years after the war seeking to discover the fate of her agents.

## Villains, allies and others

'It is so difficult to make these villains frightening,' Fleming observed. 'But one is ashamed to overwrite them though that is probably what the public would like.' No one ever accused Fleming of *under*writing his villains, who are as lurid and sensational as Bond himself is deliberately understated. They are all extraordinary – ugly, deformed, brilliant, sadistic, rich, power-mad and unrepentantly insane. 'So was Frederick the Great,' crows Ernst Stavro Blofeld. 'So was Nietzsche, so was Van Gogh. We are in good, illustrious company…' Many have specific physical characteristics that mark them out as evil, or psychologically damaged, and usually both: an absence of earlobes, a gap between the front teeth, even red hair. Most are foreign, and a large proportion are German or Russian. Many are overweight, some astonishingly so – Blofeld tips the scales at thirty stone; several are wildly camp (Le Chiffre in *Casino Royale* addresses Bond as 'dear boy', Noël Coward's favourite form of address); Rosa Klebb is a lesbian; several villains are homosexual; and one is apparently an extreme opera fan – we meet Blofeld in *You Only Live Twice* dressed as a Valkyrie, complete with chainmail. These were not qualities, to put it mildly, that Fleming admired. Although some of Fleming's close friends were homosexual, he shared the prejudices of his time and class, and so does Bond. Fleming's villains do nothing by halves. Blofeld's criminal enterprises are 'on a scale of a Caligula, of a Nero, of a Hitler, of any of the greatest enemies of mankind'. Fleming's villains emerged out of a postwar world that had just witnessed, and defeated, wickedness on an unimaginable scale; yet some of the perpetrators of that evil – Mengele, Bormann and others – were still believed to be at large, and assumed to be living a life of criminal luxury. The criminal inventiveness of Bond's enemies seemed horribly believable in a world that had experienced the death camps, Japanese torture and Gestapo interrogation methods. Bond refers to friends who have been tortured during the war, and Fleming's personal knowledge of what could happen to captured agents again underpins the fiction. 'You only have to read about the many tortures used in the war by the Germans which were practised on several of our agents to realise that mine is mild stuff compared with that,' he once said.

Most of Bond's enemies are older, male, super-rich and sophisticated, a pattern that has prompted some to see Fleming's villains as caricatures of patriarchal figures. And it is certainly true that Bond is repeatedly brought to the villain's lair, told he is a young fool, and then prepared for punishment. This was a scene only too

Ernst Stavro Blofeld (played by Donald Pleasence), Fleming's arch-villain, pictured here with his white Persian cat, an accoutrement that never appears in any of the books.

familiar to Fleming from many unpleasant encounters with his cane-wielding housemaster at Eton, and to any number of ex-public-schoolboys familiar with corporal punishment. 'My dear boy,' Le Chiffre spoke, like a father, 'the game of Red Indians is over, quite over. You have stumbled by mischance into a game for grown-ups.' Bond's ability to trip up the patronising crooks and bullies had an instant appeal to every grown-up schoolboy who still dreamed of kicking the headmaster in the groin.

Once more, Fleming's villains, like his heroes, are patchworks of different people, names and traits. Le Chiffre, the sweaty, Benzedrine-sniffing villain of *Casino Royale*, is believed to be based on Aleister Crowley, who gained huge notoriety in inter-war Britain as 'The Wickedest Man in the World'. Crowley was a bisexual, sado-masochistic drug addict with the ears of a leprechaun and the eyes of a dissipated stoat. A master of Thelemic mysticism ('Do what thou wilt shall be the whole of the Law'), he specialised in mountaineering, interpreting the Ouija board, orgies and thrashing his lovers. The press simultaneously adored and hated him. Crowley made Le Chiffre seem positively sane.

Oddly enough, Crowley is also claimed to have been a British spy. The *International Journal of Intelligence and Counterintelligence* recorded that, while living in America during the First World War, Crowley used the cover of a German propagandist to gather information for the British secret service on the German intelligence network in the United States, and on Irish Republican activity. During the Second World War, Crowley personally offered to make contact with Rudolf Hess, Hitler's deputy, who was thought to be fascinated by the occult. After Hess landed in Scotland, Crowley offered to intercede as a sort of mystical go-between: 'If it is true that Herr Hess is much influenced by Astrology and magick, my services might be of use,' he wrote. Fleming was clearly intrigued, and suggested using Crowley to supply Hess with fake horoscopes, or as an interrogator. After all, Crowley and Hess spoke the same language, namely gobbledegook. Neither idea came to fruition, but Crowley had plainly made a strong impression.

Fleming plundered his school register ruthlessly in the quest for names. Hugo Drax, the villain in *Moonraker*, was named after the magnificently festooned Admiral Sir Reginald Aylmer Ranfurly Plunkett-Ernle-Erle-Drax, an acquaintance of Fleming's who led the pre-war military mission to Moscow in 1939 to discuss a possible alliance with the USSR. Ernst Stavro Blofeld, the super-villain without earlobes (he also has no cats in the novels; that had to wait for the movies), was probably named after another Old Etonian, Tom Blofeld, a farmer from Norfolk whose son Henry Blofeld is the much-loved, plummy-voiced BBC cricket

Aleister Crowley, occultist, mystic, drug addict and sexual omnivore, was the 'wickedest man in England', according to his detractors. He may also have been the inspiration for Le Chiffre, the villain of *Casino Royale*.

commentator. Alternatively, Blofeld may owe his name to China scholar John Blofeld, who was a member of Fleming's club, Boodles, and whose father was named Ernst. Red Grant, the assassin in *From Russia with Love*, was the name of a cheerful river guide Fleming knew in Jamaica, and Francisco 'Pistols' Scaramanga, the triple-nippled gunman in *The Man with the Golden Gun*, was named after yet another school contemporary, George Scaramanga. Fleming and Scaramanga are said to have had a number of schoolyard fights. Fleming got his revenge in print. (The original Scaramanga had the regulation number of nipples.)

While most of Fleming's friends and acquaintances enjoyed appearing in the series, a few objected vehemently. In *Diamonds Are Forever*, Fleming described the homosexual villain 'Boofy' Kidd: 'Kidd's a pretty boy. His friends call him "Boofy"…some of these homos make the worst killers.' This was all very well, but one of Fleming's best friends (and a relative of his wife, Ann) was Arthur Gore, later the Earl of Arran, who was universally known by the distinctive nickname 'Boofy'. Gore was livid and complained bitterly, to no avail.

Another who strongly objected to seeing his name in a Bond novel was Ernö Goldfinger, the distinguished and controversial modernist architect. Fleming first heard the name from his golfing partner,

John Blackwell, who was a cousin by marriage of Ernö Goldfinger and disliked him. Fleming is said to have objected to Goldfinger's love of concrete and the destruction of Victorian houses to make way for his tower blocks. According to one theory, Fleming particularly hated a terrace of modern houses designed by Goldfinger on Willow Road in Hampstead, and so used his name for one of his most memorable evildoers: Auric Goldfinger, the richest man in England; treasurer of the Soviet counter-intelligence agency, SMERSH; and a gold-obsessive who likes to paint his lovers with gold in order to make love to the substance he craves. When Ernö obtained a proof copy of *Goldfinger*, he gave it to his associate, Jacob Blacker, and asked him whether he should sue. Blacker read the book and reported that the only substantial difference was: 'You're called Ernö and he's called Auric.' This was rather rude, since Ernö was a visionary six-foot architect and Auric is a murderous five-foot megalomaniac. But, unlike most of Fleming's name-borrowings, there are a few genuine similarities between the Goldfingers: both were Jewish émigrés from Eastern Europe who liked fast cars, and both were Marxists, in Auric's case by association with SMERSH. There is also a whiff of anti-Semitism in Fleming's depiction of a Jewish billionaire with a gold fixation. The real Goldfinger was exceptionally unamused, summoned his lawyers, and threatened to halt publication. Equally angry, Fleming thought his publisher should insert an erratum slip, changing Goldfinger to 'Goldprick' throughout the book (a name originally suggested, unseriously, by the critic Cyril Connolly). A truce was established after Fleming's publishers agreed that, in advertising the book, the name Goldfinger would be coupled with the name Auric wherever possible. Even so, for the rest of his life Ernö Goldfinger was plagued by people calling him on the telephone and saying, in the voice of Sean Connery, 'Goldfinger? This is 007.'

Ernö provided the name, unwittingly and unwillingly, but the character of Goldfinger may have been based on the extrovert and flashy American gold tycoon Charles W. Engelhard Jr, whom Fleming met in 1949 and remained friends with. Engelhard was owner of a huge mining and metals conglomerate, and a major racehorse owner. The gold magnate delighted in the general assumption that he was the inspiration for Goldfinger, turning up to parties dressed in orange and pretending that he had a stewardess named Pussy Galore on his private plane.

'Q', the head of research and development for the secret service and irascible provider of Bond's gadgets and cars, would become a staple character in the films, but there is no Q character in the books. In *Casino Royale*, Bond is told to 'see Q for any equipment you need', but this is most likely to be a reference to 'Q-Branch', the real name of a shadowy department which supplied uniforms, gizmos and other unconventional weapons of war. Charles Fraser-Smith of Q-Branch had provided much of the equipment for Operation Ruthless, Fleming's aborted plan to capture the Enigma codebook. A former missionary in Morocco, Fraser-Smith was nominally a civil servant with the Ministry of Supply's Clothing and Textile Department, under cover of which he made equipment for secret agents, saboteurs and prisoners of war, such as miniature cameras, maps written in invisible ink and golf balls hollowed out to hide a compass. When this latter technique was used to conceal diamonds in the film of *Diamonds Are Forever*, Fraser-Smith was critical, pointing out that the golf balls he had designed during the war were ideal secret receptacles since they would still work as golf balls, whereas those imagined in the film would barely have got off the ground.

Fleming clearly derived great pleasure, and considerable devilry, from his choice of names, whether the subject was good, bad or inanimate. He had an extraordinary ear for names with a ring to them, a gift which later imitators have found hard to emulate. 'He took immense trouble with names and plots, although the names sometimes came before the plots,' said his friend Ivar Bryce (whose own name would be adopted by Bond as an alias in *Live and Let Die*). 'He enjoyed using the names of his friends, or even those he only knew slightly.' Or not at all. People were named after things, and things were named after people. His lover in later life, Blanche Blackwell, gave him a small boat named *Octopussy*, which became the name of a man-eating pet octopus in the short story. In rather ungallant return, Fleming named the ancient guano tanker in *Dr No* the *Blanche*. The crime boss Marc-Ange Draco in *On Her Majesty's Secret Service* is named after El Draco, the Spanish name for the English privateer Sir Francis Drake – a reference picked up years later by J. K. Rowling for her Hogwarts antihero, Draco Malfoy. Rosa Klebb (the Russian for bread) was partly based on Colonel Rybkin of Soviet intelligence. Major Boothroyd, the secret service armourer, is named in honour of Geoffrey Boothroyd, the gun expert who provided Fleming with invaluable technical advice. Ernie Cuneo, a hard-nosed New York lawyer and friend of Fleming, found himself turned into Ernie Cureo, the Las Vegas taxi-driver and undercover CIA agent in *Diamonds Are Forever*; his American friends Tommy and Oatsie Leiter became Felix Leiter, Bond's CIA ally. One of the more charming christenings was that of Vesper Lynd in *Casino Royale*. One afternoon in Jamaica, Fleming and Ivar Bryce visited a romantically isolated mansion on the coast and were ushered in to meet 'The Colonel'. A little later, a dusty butler appeared and announced, 'Vespers are served', while dishing up a powerful concoction of rum, herbs, fruit and ice. Ever after, Fleming associated the word Vesper with a heady sort of glamour, and made her Bond's first lover. Darko Kerim, the extrovert secret service agent in *From Russia with Love*, was based on Nazim Kalkavan, Fleming's guide to Istanbul when he covered an Interpol conference there in 1956.

Fleming teased his friends and acquaintances by putting them, their names, or their characteristics in his books. But the character he most pillaged for material was himself. It is a measure of Fleming's introspection that he could identify his own virtues as well as his vices, and inject them both into the personality of James Bond. In Bond's obituary in *The Times*, from *You Only Live Twice*, Fleming cannot resist the opportunity to write his own epitaph, with a knowing glimmer of self-congratulation:

> To serve the confidential nature of his work, he was accorded the rank of lieutenant in the Special Branch of the RNVR, and it is a measure of the satisfaction his services gave to his superiors that he ended the war with the rank of commander.

# 004

## THE PLOTS:
## FROM HOT WAR TO COLD WAR

the entire structure of British intelligence. For most of the war, Britain had conducted the espionage battle against Germany with remarkable results; by 1952, the conductor's baton had passed to the US, and Britain was firmly in the position of second fiddle.

Ian Fleming simply ignored this inconvenient fact. His fantasy of an omnipotent British secret service nourished millions of readers on both sides of the Atlantic, and spread a legend of British espionage efficiency that persists to this day. In a now-notorious speech of 2003, President George W. Bush implicitly summoned up the ghost of James Bond when he cited British intelligence as a reason for invading Iraq: 'The British government has learned that Saddam Hussein recently sought significant quantities of uranium from Africa.' French spy work, say, or even American intelligence, would not have carried quite the same cachet. The information about African uranium was wrong, but that is not the point here: Fleming and Bond spread the belief that Britain produced the best spies in the world and, bizarrely, the myth stuck.

Fleming's characters and plots emerge, in many instances, directly from the Second World War. Even the demonology derives from that conflict: evildoers being, in approximate order of untrustworthiness, German, Russian, Japanese, Bulgarian, Korean and French. Characters are endowed with realistic, and often elaborate, past histories, to place them more firmly in the present. Polish-born Blofeld, we discover, spied for Germany during the war. The brutal communist Le Chiffre was found wandering in the Dachau displaced persons camp, apparently suffering from amnesia. He has no name; he is merely the number, 'le chiffre'. The ghastly Rosa Klebb, the colonel in charge of operations and executions for SMERSH, is given an earlier career in the Spanish Civil War, working for Andrés Nin, the Spanish communist revolutionary. Nin was tortured and murdered, on Stalin's orders, in 1937. Fleming implies that his murderer was the fictional Klebb.

Many of the names chosen by Fleming were German, an unsubtle code to indicate that the Nazi menace was still at large: Egon Bartsch and Dr Walter are German scientists who worked on the Nazi rocket programme employed by Drax on the Moonraker project; Bruno Bayer is a former Gestapo agent now working for SPECTRE. Drax himself is really former Nazi officer Graf Hugo von der Drache ('Drache' being German for dragon), and his aide de camp is Willy Krebs, a name at least some of Fleming's readers would have recognised – General Hans Krebs was Hitler's army chief of staff, who committed suicide in the Führer's bunker shortly after Hitler himself.

The nuclear bomb from *Octopussy* (1983).

Bond's allies have seen war service: Leiter is a former captain with the US Marines; in *Moonraker*, 008 has returned from Peenemunde, site of the wartime rocket research facility in northern Germany; even Mary Goodnight, Bond's secretary, is an ex-Wren. Bond was born at a time when memoirs and biographies of Second World War personalities were being published in large numbers, revealing a real world of derring-do that came as a revelation to many readers. That individuals had carried out acts of unbelievable bravery in the war made Bond that much more believable. The Second World War provides the psychological backdrop for almost all the principal characters. 'He was back there again fighting war,' Fleming writes of Tiger Tanaka, the spy trained as a kamikaze pilot who heads the Japanese secret service in *You Only Live Twice*. 'Bond knew the symptoms. He often visited this haunted forest of memory himself.' Or as Bond remarks in *Thunderball*: 'The war just doesn't seem to have ended for us.'

The clues to the Second World War are everywhere, yet Bond is fighting an emphatically new war, against a looming communist threat, in the shape of its most evil and ruthless manifestation, SMERSH. Once again, Fleming drew on reality and reshaped it to lend credibility to this imagined combat. The people, the weapons, the scenes, all carried deliberate echoes of real wartime events. The underwater trap door in the hull of the *Disco Volante* in *Thunderball* and the limpet-mining of Mr Big's boat in *Live and Let Die* may well be based on the extraordinary wartime activities of the 10th Light Flotilla, an elite unit of Italian navy frogmen, who used similar methods to attack Allied shipping off Gibraltar in what Fleming considered 'the greatest piece of effrontery in the underwater war'. The assassination attempt on Bond in *Casino Royale* was, according to Fleming himself, based on the attempted Soviet assassination in 1942 of the former spymaster Franz von Papen, then Germany's ambassador to Turkey: in both fact and fiction, the assassins were Bulgarians acting as Soviet agents, and in both cases they failed to kill the target and blew themselves up instead.

If some of Fleming's plots transposed Second World War events into a Cold War setting, others were drawn directly from the events of the Cold War itself. Real people, such as Lavrenty Beria, chief of Soviet security and one of Stalin's principal executioners, are mentioned to lend authenticity: the fall of Beria (executed on the orders of Khrushchev in 1953) enables Grubozaboyschikov to become head of SMERSH and allows Rosa Klebb to take over Otydel II, in charge of operation and execution. Interestingly, Fleming states that Beria 'went to the gallows' on 13 January 1954, the official Soviet date of the execution; after the

The Cuban Missile Crisis: a low-level photograph from 1962 of a medium-range ballistic missile site at Sagua La Grande, Cuba, showing launch erectors removed and the launch pads bulldozed over.

files were later opened, however, it was revealed that Beria had been shot almost a month earlier. Such mingling of fact and fiction is deliberate and highly effective. Fleming occupied a world radically divided between the communist East and the capitalist West, and one that was intensely paranoid. The *Thunderball* plot imagined Blofeld threatening to bomb Miami with stolen atomic weapons, eerily foreshadowing the 1962 Cuban Missile Crisis. To contemporary readers, that menace seemed only too real. Indeed, the failure of the Bay of Pigs invasion and the Cuban crisis reinforced fear of the Soviet threat, and boosted the sales of Fleming's books.

Indeed, for a time Bond was physically as close to the action of the Cold War as it was possible to get: namely, on the bedside table of the President of the United States. John F. Kennedy was first introduced to Fleming's books in 1955, and read a copy of *Casino Royale* while convalescing in New England. He remained a fan to the end of his life. In 1961, Kennedy named *From Russia with Love* in his top ten favourite books, an endorsement that did no harm to his image, and did wonders for Fleming's US sales. A subsequent advertisement featured a picture of the White House with a single window lit and the caption: 'You can bet on it he's reading one of those Ian Fleming thrillers.' The enthusiasm

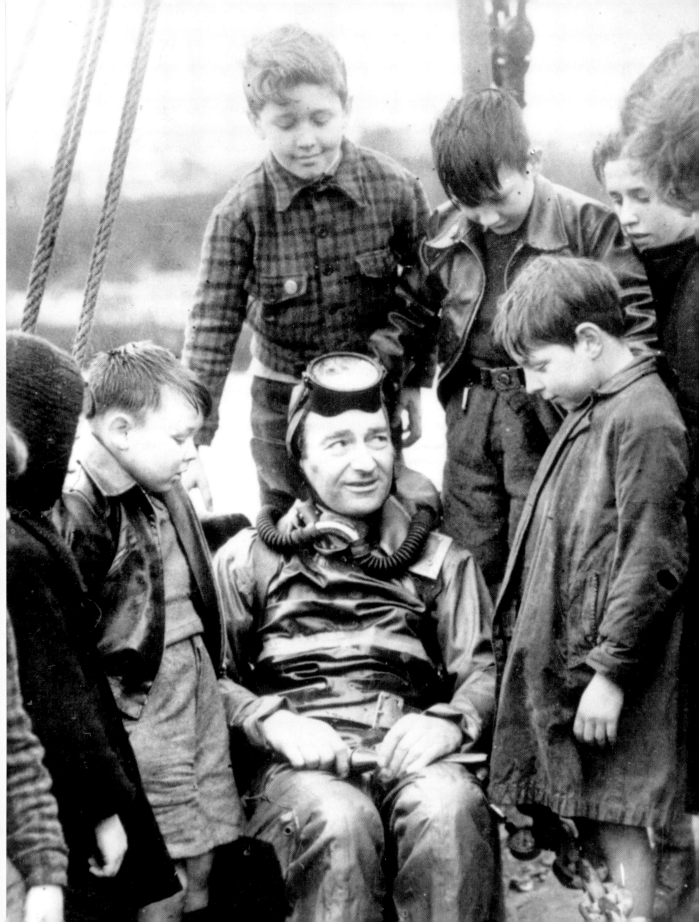

Crabb will for ever be linked with the more outlandish antics of the British secret service. In 1956, this Royal Navy frogman was recruited by MI6 to inspect the hull of the Soviet cruiser that had brought Nikita Khrushchev on a state visit to Britain. Crabb's mission was probably to search for mine-laying hatches and sonar equipment on the bottom of the Soviet ship as it lay in Portsmouth harbour. The MI6 officer in charge of the mission was Nicholas Elliott, a friend of Fleming's. Crabb was unfit; the mission was idiotic, diplomatically unwise and exceedingly dangerous. It was, needless to say, a disaster. Crabb's headless body was found off the coast fourteen months later. The Crabb affair prompted outrage, a diplomatic firestorm, the resignation of MI6 director John Sinclair, and a flood of speculation that continues unabated. But it proved to the public that the British secret service was still capable of the most extravagant adventures. Three years later, Fleming sent Bond out to investigate the hull of the *Disco Volante* in *Thunderball*; unlike Crabb, he returns intact, just.

If Crabb was the Western spy who failed, then Nikolai Khokhlov was the Soviet spy who very nearly succeeded. A KGB spy whose exploits rival any of the models on which Bond was based, Khokhlov had fought behind the lines in the Second World War, and had taken part in the assassination of the Nazi official Wilhelm Kube, then Generalkommissar for White Russia. Khokhlov's spymaster was Pavel Sudoplatov, head of the Administration for Special Tasks in the NKVD (which would become the KGB), in charge of sabotage and assassinations. From the seventh floor of the dreaded Lubyanka building, Sudoplatov plotted the deaths of those perceived as enemies of the regime, including the murder of Trotsky in 1940. In 1953, Khokhlov was selected by Sudoplatov to assassinate a prominent anti-Soviet Russian émigré in Berlin. Khokhlov, a man of conscience, found he could not carry out such a murder in cold blood, and instead defected to the West, bringing with him an extraordinary array of murderous gadgetry, including two guns housed in metal cigarette cases, which could fire up to four hollow steel bullets, and a miniature revolver that fired poisoned bullets. Khokhlov's defection was a sensation, but perhaps still more astounding was the Soviet riposte: in 1957, while attending a conference in Frankfurt, Khokhlov drank a cup of coffee that had been laced with radioactive thallium. Its effects were terrifying. Khokhlov's face erupted in black, brown and blue lumps, his eyes oozed a sticky liquid and his hair fell out in handfuls. The blood in his veins began to turn to plasma, as his bones crumbled. Astonishingly, Khokhlov survived, thanks to repeated transfusions by American doctors working around the clock. Khokhlov was still alive when

Commander Lionel 'Buster' Crabb, the naval war hero whose headless body was found more than a year after he was sent by MI6 to inspect the hull of a Soviet cruiser – provoking a political furore and inspiring the plot of *Thunderball*.

this book was being written, living in quiet retirement in San Bernardino, California, an astonishing monument to Soviet ruthlessness and his own resilience. Khokhlov's remarkable book, *In the Name of Conscience*, was published in 1959. A copy inevitably found its way on to Fleming's bookshelves, and from there into his fiction. The gun concealed inside a copy of *War and Peace* and wielded by the Soviet assassin Red Grant in *From Russia with Love* owed its inception to the Khokhlov haul of assassination gadgetry. In an interview in 2006, Khokhlov told me: 'The KGB decided to kill me… From this moment there was a general direction to hunt Khokhlov. The message was: "We will get the traitor, wherever he is in the world."' This, of course, was precisely the role of SMERSH, both in Fleming's books, and in reality.

Thanks to James Bond, SMERSH became a household name, but few realise that such an organisation really existed, long before Fleming gave it wicked immortality. In the bewildering forest of acronyms that was the Soviet secret service, SMERSH was just one of many names by which the specialised counter-intelligence department of the Soviet Union was known. SMERSH, as Fleming writes, is formed by combining the Russian words '*Smyert*' and '*Shpionam*', meaning (approximately) 'death to spies'. Within Soviet intelligence, this unit (which would

Nikolai Khokhlov, still hairless from the effects of radioactive poisoning caused when his coffee was laced with thallium – a revenge attack eerily reminiscent of the more recent murder of former KGB officer Aleksandr Litvinenko.

The cache of Soviet espionage gadgets brought to the West by defector Nikolai Khokhlov, including a cigarette case adapted to fire toxic bullets.

Russian mafia bosses, as well as the lone maverick megalomaniacs, Osama bin Ladens *avant la lettre*. Bond's evolution from Cold War warrior to international crime-fighter reflects the changing preoccupations of the times, but also Fleming's need to ensure that beneath the fantasy lay a realistic foundation: here were new battles, with new enemies that Bond and Britain could realistically fight and, more importantly, defeat.

Unlike his film incarnation, Bond is not immune to doubt, but the moments when he is on the back foot are rare indeed: his is a universe where Britain triumphs, America follows, the British secret service is supreme, communists and criminals are defeated, and the globe is a better place for it. One may dismiss all of this as propagandist fantasy (many did just that, particularly on the other side of the Iron Curtain), but the world Fleming described was, in some deeper sense than mere reality, true. In the real world, secret agents did not go around sticking limpet mines on ships, torturing their enemies, or killing one another with poisoned bullets fired from cigarette cases. Except that they did, and they still do. As you read this, secret agents are working undercover to track down individuals mad enough to threaten the world by stealing atomic missiles or threatening biological warfare, in the manner of Blofeld. The fear of weapons of mass destruction permeates our world, just as it runs through the Bond books. And in London, an outspoken Russian defector dies after agents unknown slip radioactive poison into his food.

How much of James Bond is true? Fleming himself joked that 'if the quality of these books, or their degree of veracity, had been any higher, the author would have certainly been prosecuted under the Official Secrets Act'. Perhaps the most pleasing irony is that, even today, MI6 itself is a little ambivalent about where James Bond ends and real life begins. The official MI6 website (www.sis.gov.uk) asks, 'How realistic is the depiction of SIS in the James Bond films?' but then only half-answers the question. 'James Bond, as Ian Fleming originally conceived him, was based on reality… But any author needs to inject a level of glamour and excitement beyond reality in order to sell.' Yet the spy agency cannot bring itself to deny its greatest asset. 'Nevertheless,' continues the article, 'staff who join SIS can look forward to a career that will have moments when the gap narrows just a little and the certainty of a stimulating and rewarding career which, like Bond's, will be in the service of their country.'

James Bond is now an MI6 recruiter. A real spy agency, harnessing fiction, based on fact, to recruit real spies: no one would have been more flattered than Ian Fleming.

Fleming was increasingly in demand as an espionage expert. As this telegram shows, the features editor of *Esquire* was willing to pay good money, even if he could not spell the author's name correctly.

POST **GPO** OFFICE

CABLE & WIRELESS

SERVICES

VIA IMPERIAL

ISSUING OFFICE—LONDON

IN 13    16 36

IN 13    16 19    D    2431

RECEIVED
PARTICULARS

The first line of this Telegram contains the following particulars in the order named :
Prefix Letters and Number of Message, Office of Origin, Number of Words, Date, Time handed in and Official Instructions, if any.

CW

GWB172 GB QA86  VU TWXC5

NEWYORK 45 13 1049A EDT

IAN FLEMMING LONDON TIMES LONDON

WOULD YOU WRITE THIRTY FIVE HUNDRED WORD ARTICLE ON

RUSSIAN  ESPIONAGE MISTAKES SINCE END WORLD WAR 11

STOP NEED BY JULY FIRST STOP WILL PAY EIGHT HUNDRED

FIFTY  DOLLARS WOULD APPRECIATE IMMEDIATE REPLY

REGARDS CLAY FELKER    FEATURES EDITOR ESQUIRE

MAGAZINE    should be accompanied by this form.    Mark your reply VIA IMPERIAL

COLL 11

# 005

## GADGETS, GUNS, GIZMOS AND GEAR-STICKS

Ian Fleming understood the extraordinary attraction of 'things'. Not
just material things (though Bond certainly appreciated those),
but things that did things, for the 1950s was the great age of the
machine: cars, domestic appliances, trains, planes, space-saving
devices; machines to make life easier, faster and also, in the case
of ever more sophisticated weapons, shorter. This was an age when
domestic appliances – food mixers, teasmaids, televisions, fridges –
were arriving in British homes in ever-increasing numbers.

Fleming adored gadgets. He was forever on the lookout for new
inventions and new ideas, an interest reflected in his growing book
collection with its emphasis on inventions and ideas that changed the
world. When he took over the Atticus column at the *Sunday Times*, he
rather pointedly changed the title from 'People' to 'People and Things'.
His love of cars was legendary and, occasionally, life-threatening. In his
flat in Ebury Street he created a custom-made hatch, to enable the
maid to serve food without being seen; in his bathroom, declaring a
deep aversion to baths, he installed a modern shower (then a rarity)
and a special soap dispenser. A customised object added a special
glamour: after Bond proved a commercial success, Fleming rewarded
himself with a gold typewriter, and even had a gold top made for his
Bic biro. When describing technology or modes of transport in his
books, Fleming worked hard to get the details right, and when he got
them wrong (as he not infrequently did), he was grateful to readers
for pointing out his mistakes. 'I take very great pains over the technical
and geographical background to James Bond's adventures,' he wrote.
His notebooks were filled with jottings on machines and gizmos he had
seen or heard about. Whenever possible, he consulted experts. 'Facts,'
he wrote, 'are clearer than people.' Minute technical descriptions have
since become a stock in trade of the thriller writer, but Fleming was
among the first to realise that readers (particularly male readers) have
an almost insatiable desire to be told the precise make, size, shape
and structure of every machine – even if the details are forgotten the

ABOVE

Prototypes of Rosa Klebb's famous dagger-shoes, as worn by Lotte Lenya in the 1963 film of *From Russia with Love*: elegant, and lethal.

OVERLEAF

Desmond Llewelyn as Q, the Einstein of the espionage gadget, with Pierce Brosnan in *Goldeneye* (1995).

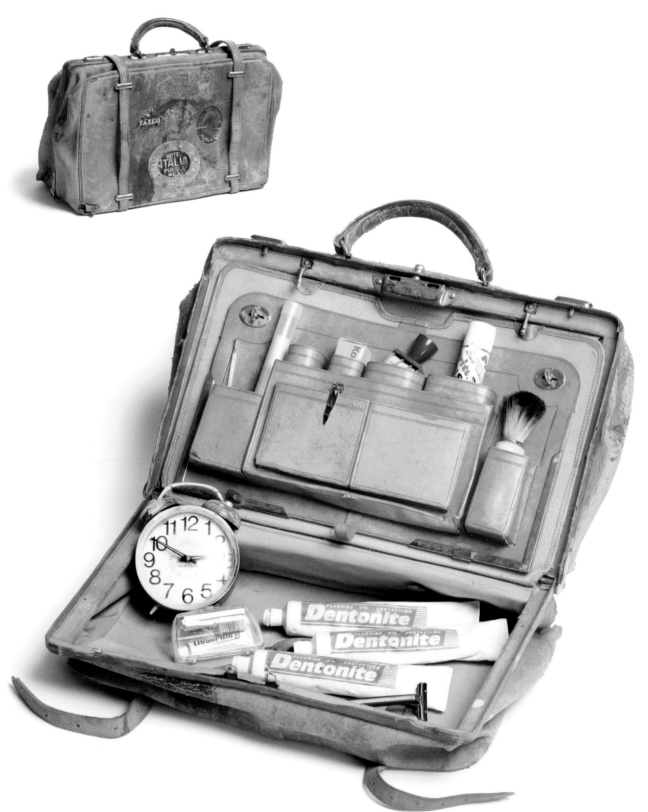

instant they are read. Fleming both shared and fed this hunger for detail: the boat owned by the villain in *Thunderball*, Emilio Largo, is no mere luxury yacht but rather a hundred-ton hydrofoil adapted from the Shertel-Sachsenberg system, with a hull of aluminium and magnesium alloy, twin Daimler-Benz four-stroke diesel engines with Brown-Boveri turbo superchargers capable of fifty knots and costing £200,000. Some machines were imaginary; most were based firmly on reality, giving the reader the important sense of being told a fiction based on truth. Kingsley Amis called this use of real information in a fictional world 'The Fleming Effect', and it proved highly successful.

Secret service gadgetry – masterminded by the irascible Q – plays a crucial role in the James Bond films, reaching almost ludicrous levels of inventiveness with flame-throwing bagpipes, exploding toothpaste and invisible cars. But gizmos are also present in the books, courtesy of Q-Branch, the genuine wartime equipment unit under the extraordinary Charles Fraser-Smith. Based in a tiny office near St James's Park, Fraser-Smith commissioned some three hundred firms around London to make an array of ingenious gadgets. He called them 'Q gadgets', after the British warships disguised as merchant vessels known as 'Q ships' in the First World War. None of the things created by Fraser-Smith was quite what it seemed: a hairbrush containing a map and a saw; magnetised matches that doubled as makeshift compasses; a pipe lined with asbestos that could be smoked without destroying the documents hidden inside (though it might well destroy the smoker); invisible ink; miniature cameras hidden in cigarette lighters; a shoelace that could also be a handy steel garrotte. Fraser-Smith was one of the great unsung lateral thinkers of the war: he devised chocolate laced with garlic so that agents dropped into France might swiftly acquire pungent breath, the better to mix with the locals, and a screw-off button with a special left-hand thread in which miniature documents could be hidden. This, he believed, would take advantage of the 'unswerving logic of the German mind', since no German would ever think of trying to unscrew something the wrong way.

Fleming worked with Fraser-Smith, and his books are peppered with references to ingenious kit. Technological wizardry is not confined to Bond and his allies: his communist and criminal enemies have an equal share of the elaborate gizmos. In *Casino Royale*, Le Chiffre conceals 'Eversharp' razor blades in his hatband, shoe heel and cigarette case; a gun hidden in an innocent-looking cane is the first method employed to try to kill Bond; and a 'small carpet of steel spikes' is used to stop

*Q's travelling case from*
*A View to a Kill.*

treasure', and he was fascinated by the 'lonely and queer' underwater world Cousteau introduced him to. Two weeks spent scuba-diving and watching Cousteau's divers at work provided him with numerous details for later books. Most immediately, the extraordinary experience of loading up with thirty pounds of equipment and slipping into the 'limitless grey depths' furnished the technical inspiration for Bond's memorable underwater adventures in *Live and Let Die*, his second novel.

Fleming's crooks also display a firm grip on high technology – high, at least, by the standards of the time. Seraffimo Spang, boss of the Spangled Mob in *Diamonds Are Forever*, has a Cadillac with the windscreen ground to the precise prescription of his glasses; this may have enabled Spang to drive without spectacles, but imagine the experience for a passenger of seeing the road coming towards you through someone else's prescription lenses. Clearly the disinclination to wear glasses was some of sort of criminal affectation in Fleming's (myopic) eyes: Dr No wears contact lenses and so does Blofeld, in the latter case tinted dark green. Contact lenses were still a new invention, the first corneal lenses having been developed as recently as 1949. Dr No has an electric razor and a clock with luminous numbers; villains use walkie-talkies; the reader's attention is drawn to such technological luxuries as the seventeen-inch television in a Las Vegas hotel room, and the oxygen bar at Santa Fe airport. Today, such things seem fairly commonplace, but to readers of Bond in the 1950s they were marks of extreme technological sophistication. Bond, for example, drinks coffee made in an American Chemex. This was a one-piece, hourglass-shaped vessel of heat-resistant glass, an all-in-one coffee filter machine with a leather collar around its waist: the filter paper went in the top, and the coffee dripped through to the bottom. As a piece of domestic engineering, it was hardly complex, but it has since become a collector's item, displayed in design museums. The Chemex was invented in 1941 by a German chemist named Peter J. Schlumbohm (the sort of name that Fleming might have noted for future use). Very few readers today would know what a Chemex is; very few readers, in fact, would have known in 1955. But Fleming had tested and tasted coffee from a Chemex. It sounded modern and scientific, and it still does; and that, perhaps, is the point.

In May 1956, Fleming received the sort of reader's letter he partly dreaded and partly appreciated: James Bond, the writer complained, 'has a rather deplorable taste in firearms'. This was not, perhaps, all that surprising, since Fleming, unlike his brother Peter, had little time or taste for guns. He still owned the Colt .38 Police Positive engraved

and presented to him by Bill Donovan, the US spy chief, but there is no evidence he ever fired it. He found the minutiae of gun science extremely boring, but as an essential element of the Bond mystique he appreciated the importance of accuracy. The letter-writer was one Geoffrey Boothroyd, a thirty-one-year-old ICI technician from Glasgow and an amateur firearms enthusiast of remarkable expertise. Boothroyd had an enormous personal collection of firearms in every shape and size, and an encyclopaedic grasp of the subject. The Beretta pistol Bond had used in the books so far was 'really a ladies' gun, and not a really nice lady at that', Boothroyd informed Fleming. In *Casino Royale*, Bond uses a Beretta in a chamois leather holster; Fleming himself had been issued with a .25 ACP Beretta during the war, and may have assumed it was the standard-issue secret agent's weapon; more likely it was simply the first gun he could think of.

Bond would be far better off, Boothroyd suggested, with a chunky Smith & Wesson .38 Centennial Airweight, a real 'man-stopper', carried in a Berns-Martin Triple-Draw holster with a built-in spring for rapid drawing. In addition, Bond should have a .357 Smith & Wesson magnum to keep in the car for shooting villains who might be further away. Fleming wrote back with polite enthusiasm, saying that Bond would certainly be pleased with his updated armoury, and adding, 'I am most anxious to see that he lives as long as possible and I shall be most grateful for any further technical advice.' There followed an extraordinarily arcane discussion about silencers: Boothroyd was against them, on the grounds that they are really the stuff of fiction. That, of course, was exactly why Fleming wanted to silence Bond's gun, and he claimed that he had used a silencer on a Sten gun during the war, which reduced the noise to a mere click. Fleming could not really care less whether a silencer worked in reality, but he needed it to work in fiction for the sake of his plots. Eventually, on Boothroyd's advice, Bond swapped his Beretta ('I am killing the bloody gun in my next book – on sound grounds') for a Walther PPK 7.65, because Boothroyd thought it was the best automatic of its size with ammunition available worldwide. With Boothroyd's help, the villains of SMERSH were kitted out, fictionally speaking, with 9mm Lugers and Mauser 7.63 automatics. Fleming swiftly got over the belief that guns were dull, and under Boothroyd's tuition became something of an expert: a staggering array of artillery is deployed in the Bond books, each described with full specifications, including a long-barrelled .45 Colt Army Special, a Savage 99F, a Winchester International Experimental .308 target rifle and a number of spear guns. Scaramanga, of course, totes a gold-plated single-action Colt .45.

Boothroyd loaned Fleming his own Smith & Wesson .38, which the artist Richard Chopping used as a model for the cover of *From Russia with Love*. Fleming's promise that this would make Boothroyd's gun 'for ever famous' was only a slight exaggeration, since the effect on its owner was exactly that. In *Dr No*, 'Major Boothroyd' is the name given to the secret service armourer, along with a flattering encomium from M: 'You may not know it, 007, but Major Boothroyd's the greatest small-arms expert in the world.' In the films, the characters of Q and Major Boothroyd are melded together, appearing in every film except *Live and Let Die* and *Casino Royale*. Boothroyd was now for ever famous.

Fleming's interest in machines found its most extreme (and expensive) expression in his love of cars. He wrote, and avidly read, motoring journalism, fell in love with cars passionately and promiscuously, and penned the most famous book about a car ever written: *Chitty Chitty Bang Bang* – published in 1964, the year of his death. Fleming himself owned a diverse succession of cars, from humble bangers as a young man to the magnificent black Ford Thunderbird he bought when he was famous, a car Ann Fleming considered 'above our price bracket and below our age range', which was probably why Ian loved it. Fleming

A poster advertising Smith & Wesson revolvers, from Fleming's personal collection of memorabilia. A Smith & Wesson .38 was drawn by artist Richard Chopping for the cover of *From Russia with Love*.

OVERLEAF
Geoffrey Boothroyd (*left*), the firearms expert who advised Fleming to re-arm James Bond with something more manly than his Beretta. He was rewarded by having his name attached to 'Major Boothroyd', Fleming's fictional secret service armourer.

# SMITH & WESSON
## All Model Circular
### Large Frame Revolvers

## The .44 Magnum*

The S & W .44 Magnum has far greater shock power than any other handgun commercially produced anywhere in the world.

| | |
|---|---|
| **CALIBER:** | .44 Magnum |
| **NUMBER OF SHOTS:** | 6 |
| **BARREL:** | 4, 6½ inches |
| **LENGTH OVER ALL:** | With 6½-inch barrel, 11⅞ inches |
| **WEIGHT:** | With 6½-inch barrel, 47 ounces |
| | With 4-inch barrel, 43 ounces |
| **SIGHTS:** | Front, ⅛-inch S & W Red Ramp; Rear, S & W Micrometer Click Sight, adjustable for windage and elevation. White Outline notch |
| **STOCKS:** | Special oversize target type, of checked Goncala Alves, with S & W monograms |
| **HAMMER:** | Checked target type |
| **TRIGGER:** | Grooved target type |
| **FINISH:** | S & W Bright Blue or Nickel |

## The ".357" Magnum*

| | |
|---|---|
| **CALIBER:** | .357 (Actual bullet diameter .38 S & W Spec.) |
| **NUMBER OF SHOTS:** | 6 |
| **BARREL:** | 3½, 5, 6, 6½, 8⅜ inches |
| **LENGTH OVER ALL:** | With 6-inch barrel, 11⅜ inches |
| **WEIGHT:** | With 8⅜-inch barrel, 47 oz., 6½-inch barrel, 44½ oz., 6-inch barrel, 44 oz., 5-inch barrel, 42½ oz., 3½-inch barrel, 41 oz. |
| **SIGHTS:** | Choice of any S & W target sights. S & W Micrometer Click rear sight, adjustable for windage and elevation |
| **STOCKS:** | Checked walnut Magna with S & W monograms |
| **FINISH:** | S & W Bright Blue or Nickel |
| **FRAME:** | ".357" Magnum, with finely checked top strap matching barrel rib. Front and rear straps, S & W grooving |

## The Highway Patrolman

| | |
|---|---|
| **CALIBER:** | .357 (Actual bullet diameter .38 S & W Spec.) |
| **NUMBER OF SHOTS:** | 6 |
| **BARREL:** | 4 or 6 inches only |
| **LENGTH OVER ALL:** | With 6-inch barrel, 11¼ inches |
| **WEIGHT:** | With 4-inch barrel, 41¾ ounces; With 6-inch barrel, 44 ounces |
| **SIGHTS:** | Front, ⅛-inch Baughman Quick Draw on plain ramp; Rear, S & W Micrometer Click sight adjustable for windage and elevation |
| **STOCKS:** | Checked walnut with S & W monograms (Magna standard, Target stocks at additional cost); Grooved tangs and trigger |
| **FINISH:** | S & W Satin Blue with Sandblast stippling on barrel top and frame edging |

## The .38/44 Heavy Duty and The 1950 Model .44 Military

| | .38/44 H. D. | .44 Mil. |
|---|---|---|
| **CALIBER:** | .38 S & W Special | .44 S & W Special |
| **NUMBER OF SHOTS:** | 6 | 6 |
| **BARREL:** | 4, 5 and 6½ inches | 4, 5 and 6½ inches |
| **LENGTH OVER ALL:** | With 5-inch barrel, 10⅜ inches | With 6½-inch barrel, 11¾ inches |
| **WEIGHT:** | With 5-inch barrel, 40 ounces | With 6½-inch barrel, 39½ ounces |
| **SIGHTS:** | Fixed, 1/10-inch service type front; square notch rear | |
| **STOCKS:** | Checked walnut Magna with S & W monograms | |
| **FINISH:** | S & W Blue or Nickel | |

**BRIGHT BLUE OR NICKEL**
**$140.00**

AMMUNITION: .44 Magnum
.44 S & W Special
.44 S & W Russian

*Reg. U. S. Pat. Office

**BRIGHT BLUE OR NICKEL**
**$120.00**

AMMUNITION: .357 S & W Magnum
.38 S & W Special Hi-Speed
.38 S & W Special
.38 S & W Special Mid Range

*Reg. U. S. Pat. Office

**BLUE ONLY**
with Magna stocks
**$85.00**

with Target stocks
**$90.00**

AMMUNITION: .357 S & W Magnum
.38 S & W Special Hi-Speed
.38 S & W Special
.38 S & W Special Mid Range

**BLUE**
**$75.00**

**NICKEL**
**$84.00**

| | .38/44 | .44 |
|---|---|---|
| AMMUNITION: | .38 S & W Special Hi-Speed | .44 S & W Special |
| | .38 S & W Special | .44 S & W Russian |
| | .38 S & W Special Mid Range | |

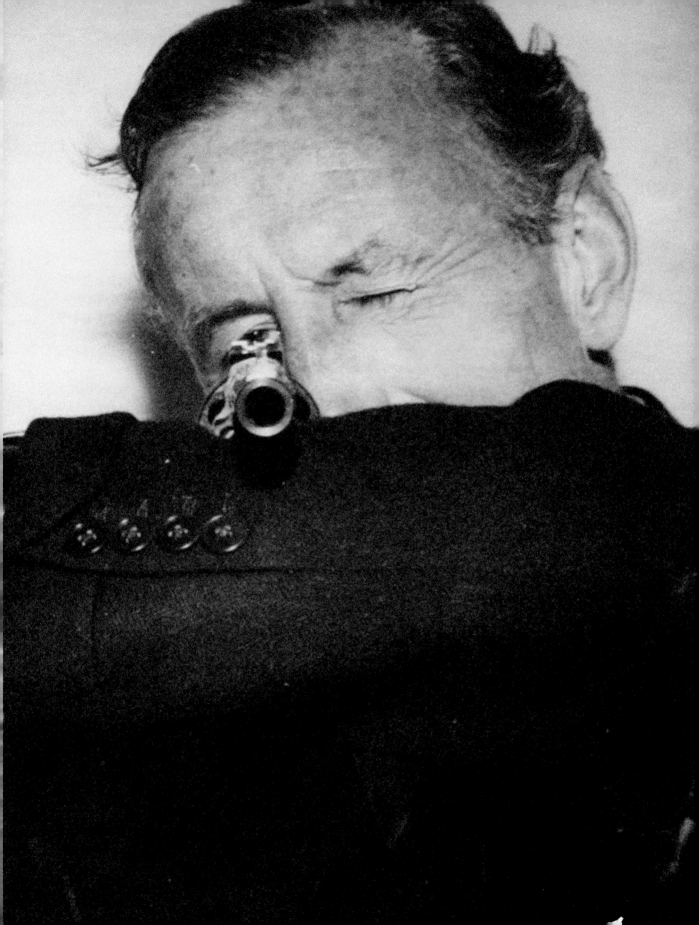

HUMAN
TRANSPLANT ORGAN
(ELECTRICALLY SUSTAINED)

HANDLE LIKE EGGS

that can change colour to provide disguise in the event of a night-time chase, a radio receiver, reinforced bumpers and a Colt .45 in a secret compartment. In the films, Bond's cars are fitted with every sort of device, starting in 1963 with a car phone (then the height of luxury and cutting-edge sophistication), and going on to include ejector seats, tyre-shredders, weapons systems, anti-pursuit mechanisms, and so on. Both Fleming and Bond took pleasure in modifying cars, and in *Chitty Chitty Bang Bang* Fleming invented the ultimate convertible. Yet both loved cars less for their accoutrements than for the pure pleasure of driving, the 'fine, deep exhaust note'. For Fleming, cars meant style and escapism; for Bond, the mighty Bentley is 'his only personal hobby'.

Fleming's knowledge of gadgets and machines was more than merely a boyish enthusiasm for technology. By anchoring his fiction in things he had seen, used, driven and researched, the author placed Bond firmly in a high-tech, glamorous reality. Readers could sense that just as Bond came from somewhere real, so the weapons he uses and the cars he drives have a provenance, albeit an exclusive one, in the real world. As a collector of facts and things and people, Fleming knew that the essence of excitement was to convince the reader of an underlying authenticity. 'I do take a lot of my plots from life,' he said. 'They are certainly bizarre, but they are also made up of real things.'

The heart transplant unit for smuggling diamonds in *The Living Daylights* (1987).

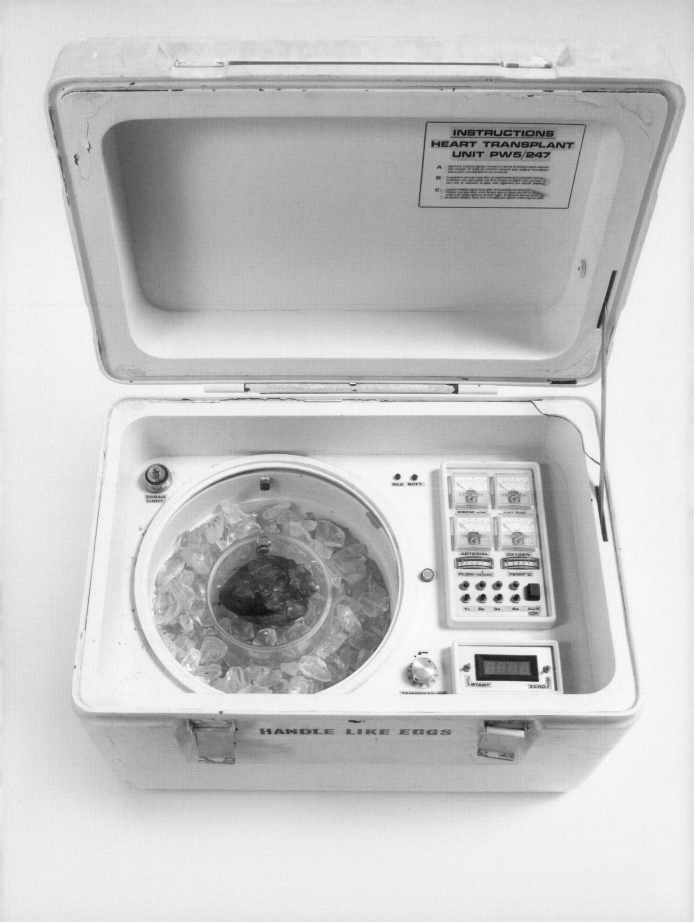

# 006

BOND GIRLS

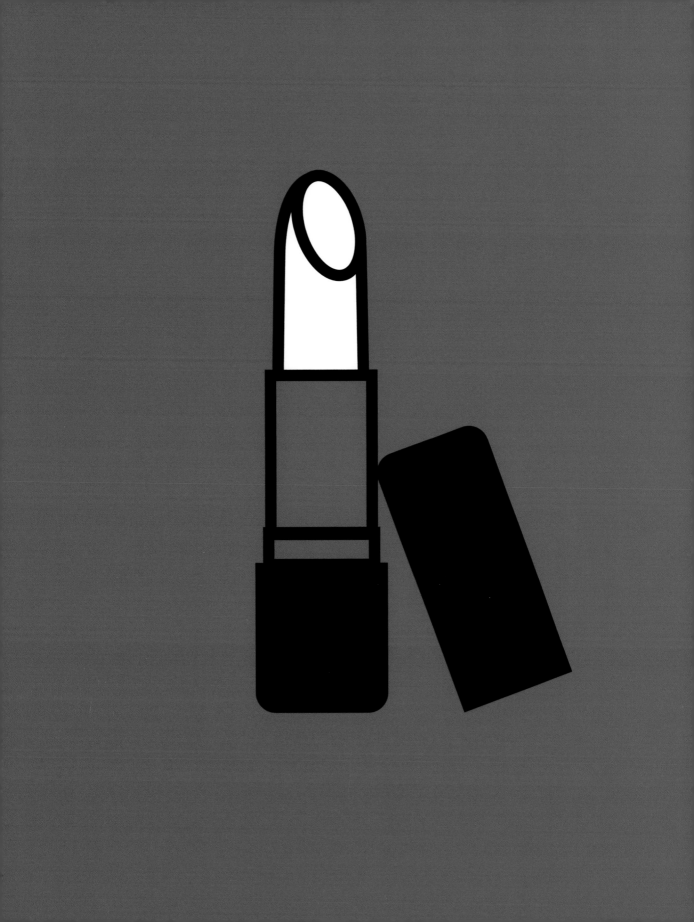

006
Bond Girls

It is a mark of James Bond's cultural reach that, for better or worse, a 'Bond Girl' has attained a specific meaning in modern parlance, with either positive or negative connotations depending on your point of view (and, perhaps, your gender). A Bond Girl is beautiful, for sure, and sassy and sporty; she is also sexually available, and unlikely to make a fuss when killed off, either literally or metaphorically, at the end of the last instalment to make way for a new love interest. She tends to be good at one-liners, but less inclined to intellectual conversation. In the books, at least, Bond's women are often damaged, in need of male protection, and have some small physical flaw. Like Bond's cars, they are attractive commodities, subject to modifications and improvements, but they can also be exchanged for newer, faster models without much regret. The Bond Girl is a very specific postwar fantasy. Fleming had enjoyed an expansive sex life before the war, but the war had loosened sexual mores greatly. Here was a hero enjoying sex, not merely outside marriage, but effectively without responsibilities or guilt.

Sex does not play a part in the lives of Bulldog Drummond or Richard Hannay. Indeed, Bond is really the first major British thriller hero to have an active sex life. Bond's attitudes to women caused outrage, titillation and amusement in roughly equal parts: they made a generation of men and boys very overexcited, and a generation of feminists extremely angry. Bond saves the girl; the girl sleeps with him: it is a simple contract. But even those critics prepared to see Bond's bed-hopping for the fantasy it was found something chilly and unpleasant in Bond's sexual licence and emotional reserve. In the films, Bond's sex life attained levels of priapism that would merit serious medical attention or industrial supplies of Viagra in a real human being. Henry Chancellor has calculated that Bond sleeps with just fourteen women in twelve books, between 1953 and 1964, of whom only five disappear between one book and the next, compared to an astonishing fifty-eight conquests in the first twenty Bond films. Readers who liked the Bond women in the books looked askance at the parade of almost

Ursula Andress on the beach in *Dr No*, wearing that bikini or, technically speaking, a black and white front-gather underwire bra with widely spaced shoulder straps and nombril bikini. And a knife.

144

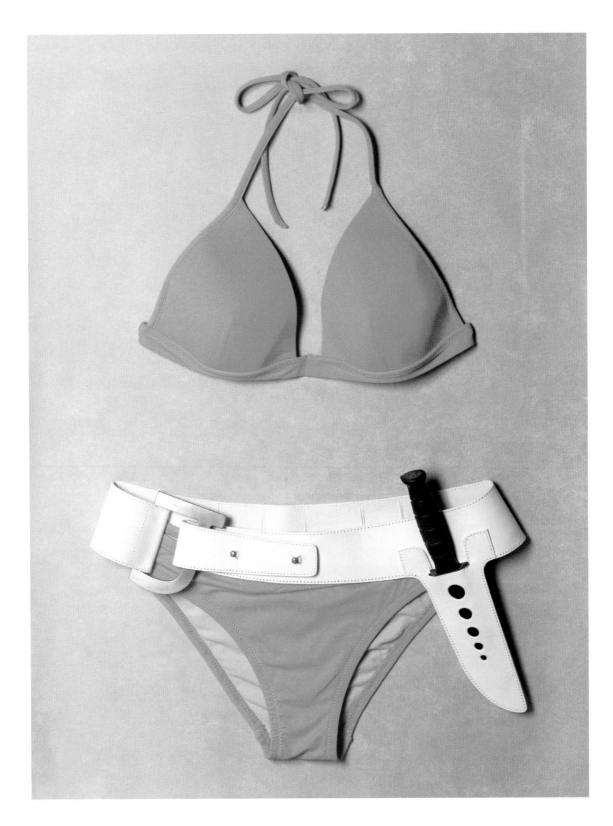

characterless beauties being loved and left in each successive film. The writer Anthony Burgess wrote that 'the girls in the Bond films tend…to be nothing more than animated centrefolds. In the books they are credible and lovable because of some humanising flaw.'

Bond's approach to sex grew directly out of Fleming's own distinctive attitudes to women, which in turn were shaped by the times he lived in, the class he occupied, and his own psychological and sexual preoccupations. Fleming might have been an easy lay, but he was not an easy man. He has sometimes, somewhat unfairly, been characterised as simply a seductive lounge lizard, a philanderer gathering sexual scalps. The truth is more complex. Fleming was certainly attracted to many women; they were attracted to him, and he knew it. His charm, wit, vulpine good looks, wealth, mysterious war record and slight air of melancholy were powerfully seductive. He had many love affairs, often with other people's wives, including those of close friends. This was not because Fleming had a particular penchant for adultery: divorce was less prevalent then, and adultery more common. Sometimes these affairs were long-lasting, but mostly they were not. An American acquaintance was struck by his apparently clinical attitude towards women: 'He got bored with them fast and could be brutal about it. He had absolutely no jealousy. He explained to me that women were not worth that much emotion. But with it all, he had an abiding and continual interest in sex without any sense of shame or guilt.' Certainly, he was more versed in seduction than courtship. 'The direct approach to sex has become the norm,' he told one interviewer. His own approach was direct to the point of bluntness. He would ask a woman, often on slender acquaintance or first meeting, to go to bed with him; if she declined, he would simply move on, unashamed, unresentful and unembarrassed, to the next potential seductee. He was successful as often as not – odds which he seemed to find perfectly acceptable. Sex was a sort of sport, and he favoured the scattergun approach. 'He looked on women as a schoolboy does. They were remote, mysterious beings,' said one family friend. 'You will never hope to understand them, but, if you're clever, you can occasionally shoot one down.' The women with whom he developed close relationships tended to be older, and more emotionally resilient.

Fleming was tremendously interested in sex. Indeed, he studied and pursued the subject, in theory and in practice, with the same avid interest he showed in gadgetry, rocketry, science and political skulduggery. He took a close interest in French pornography, and assembled an impressive personal collection of erotica, which he liked

Bikini tribute: the orange number worn by Halle Berry in *Die Another Day* (2002), in honour of the original.

when he called, and stay away when he was seeing other women. One of his friends called her Fleming's 'slave'.

Ian enjoyed showing Mu off to his friends and annoying his family by introducing this slightly scatty beauty into weekend house parties. But he undoubtedly treated her very badly. Even though they were unofficially 'engaged', Fleming was consistently and relentlessly unfaithful to her, and, unlike some of his lovers, she minded. It is said that her lack of intellect stood in the way of his commitment, but then there is no evidence Fleming considered brains to be an attractive quality in a woman, and quite a lot to indicate otherwise. Fleming's reputation was well known to Mu's horrified family: they marked Fleming down as a bounder, and her brother Fitzherbert even turned up at Fleming's home with a horse whip, intending to administer the traditional punishment for cads, only to find that Ian and Muriel, forewarned, had headed off to the safety of Brighton for the weekend. For nine years, Mu obediently trotted after Fleming. She even got a job as a motorcycle dispatch rider working for the Admiralty when Fleming was with the Naval Intelligence Division.

Then suddenly, like some character in a Bond movie, she was dead. On 14 March 1944, Muriel Wright returned to her flat in Eaton Mews (having just delivered Fleming his weekly package of cigarettes) and went to bed. That night, there was an air raid: a chunk of flying masonry hurtled through her open window, striking Mu in the temple and killing her at once. Ian, as her only known contact, was summoned from the card table to identify the body. Fleming was distraught. He was also racked with remorse at the way he had treated her. He wore Mu's bracelet on his key ring and refused to go to the London haunts they had visited together. One of Ian's associates in 30 AU, Dunstan Curtis, remarked meanly of his mourning: 'The trouble with Ian is that you have to get yourself killed before he feels anything.' But, in truth, the death of Muriel had a profound effect on Fleming's emotions, a small effect on his behaviour, and far greater impact on his writing. Mu, he reflected sadly, had been 'too good to be true'.

The quality of being 'too good to be true' is, of course, what distinguishes the Bond Girls. Muriel Wright has a strong claim to be the *fons et origo* of the species: pliant and undemanding, beautiful but innocent, outdoorsy, physically tough, implicitly vulnerable and uncomplaining, and then tragically dead, before or soon after marriage. Bond would have married Vesper Lynd, in *Casino Royale*, but she kills herself. Ten books later, there are distinct elements of Muriel in the well-born, golden-haired Countess Teresa (Tracy) di Vicenzo, in *On Her*

Muriel Wright, Fleming's wartime lover: a model, athlete and good-time girl, who was tragically killed during the bombing of London. Fleming mourned 'Mu' deeply after her death, and perhaps modelled the archetypal Bond Girl on her.

OVERLEAF
Timothy Dalton and Maryam d'Abo go sledging in a cello case in *The Living Daylights* (1987).

Bullet-holed cello from
*The Living Daylights.*

*Majesty's Secret Service*. Bond *does* marry Tracy ('She's beautiful, in bed and out. She's adventurous, brave, resourceful. She's exciting always'), but soon afterwards she, too, perishes. Bond's distress over Tracy's corpse may be an echo of Fleming's anguish at Muriel's death so many years earlier.

A year before he had met Muriel, Fleming first laid eyes on Ann (née Charteris), the young wife of Shane, Baron O'Neill, and future wife of Esmond, Lord Rothermere, and the woman Fleming would finally marry in the same year he wrote his first Bond book. Ann was in many ways the opposite of Mu, being dark, highly intelligent, waspish, worldly, sophisticated, emotionally complex and extraordinarily good company. Ian's love affair with Ann started during the war; it continued after O'Neill's death and her marriage to Rothermere; and it lasted, tumultuously, until the end of his life. This peculiar pair had very different tastes and interests: Ann enjoyed nothing more than to gather her literary and artistic friends for an evening of bibulous back-stabbing, the sort of event that Ian cordially detested, preferring the golf course, the club, or simply his own company. Ian was hardly the marrying type. To a friend, newly betrothed in 1944, he remarked sourly, 'Well, old boy, I wish you all the luck in the world, but I can't see anything in it for me.' When Ian and Ann finally did decide to marry, on 24 March 1952, he was forty-three, she was pregnant, and he anticipated the worst. Writing to his future brother-in-law, he observed: 'We are, of course, totally unsuited… China will fly and there will be rage and tears.'

There were, indeed, ample tears and flying crockery. Ann could be wounding about Ian's writing (referring to it as 'pornography'); he, in turn, made no secret of his dislike of her literary friends, her 'harem'. After two years of marriage, he was already complaining, only half in jest: 'In the old days I demanded or perhaps pleaded for three things in a wife. She should have enough money to buy her own clothes, she should be able to make incomparable Béarnaise sauce, and she should be double-jointed. In the event I got none of these things.' The rows grew furious, and the marriage colder. Fleming conducted a long affair with a neighbour in Jamaica, Blanche Blackwell; Ann did the same with Hugh Gaitskell, leader of the Labour Party. She was jealous; he, characteristically, was not. When they were apart, they missed each other painfully, he declaring: 'I love you only in the world.' When they were together, they fought viciously and, as self-absorbed people often do, publicly. Many of their friends thought the marriage should have broken up, but somehow it did not; paradoxically, the repeatedly

*A letter written by Domino to Bond, inserted as a promotional tool into the paperback edition of* Thunderball*: 'Do please say yes' to a rendezvous, she pleads, as only a Bond Girl can.*

adulterous Fleming was wedded to the idea of matrimony. Fleming wrote every one of his Bond books while locked in this peculiar relationship, in an extraordinary torrent of creativity. Perhaps Bond was a way to escape the pains of his marriage. Once he had started writing, and suffered the sneers of Ann's literary friends, he may have been impelled to keep going in order to prove that he could out-write, out-publish and out-earn every one of them; perhaps as he felt his sexual powers waning, he poured his passion into his books, for his love of words and writing was the most constant love of his life. Whatever the reason, this strange marriage endured, producing one child, Caspar, a few good times, some very unhappy times, and a lot of excellent books.

It is tempting to see shades of Fleming's turbulent marriage in Bond's attitude to women. The 'conventional parabola' of a Bond affair, described in *Casino Royale*, is a statement of unalloyed cynicism, starting with 'sentiment, the touch of the hand', and inevitably ending with 'the final bitterness': 'The meeting at a party, the restaurant, the

OVERLEAF

Eva Green and Daniel Craig
as Vesper Lynd and James
Bond in the 2006 film of
*Casino Royale*, the biggest
box-office hit for Bond so far.

taxi, his flat, her flat, then the weekend by the sea, then the flats again, then the furtive alibis and the angry farewell on some doorstep in the rain.' Bond has no time for domesticity and marriage, 'handing out canapés in an L-shaped drawing room' – a reference to the Flemings' London house in Victoria Square. Bond points out that if he got married, he would first need to divorce himself from M and the secret service. James Bond has no children, no siblings and no parents. He leaves Kissy Suzuki pregnant in *You Only Live Twice*, but there is never a suggestion that he has any sense of paternal responsibility, or wonders about his child. He is the empty vessel into which the reader decants his or her expectations. Women, Bond declares, are for recreation; he has no desire to tote the emotional baggage that comes from a serious relationship. Tracy, the girl he does marry, is eligible precisely because she is 'a lone girl, not cluttered up with friends, relations, belongings', rather like himself. Bond's women often have interesting, independent lives and missions; they are by no means chained to the sink, but essentially they are there to be admired, saved and then slept with, in that order. Even a lesbian like Pussy Galore melts before Bond's male dominance: 'She did as she was told, like an obedient child.' Bond is adamant on one point of female gastronomy: the ideal woman needs to make a Béarnaise sauce as well as she makes love, though not, presumably, at the same time.

The qualities Bond admires are physical and practical, and certainly not a matter of character or intellect: 'Gold hair. Grey eyes. A sinful mouth. Perfect figure. And of course she's got to be witty and poised and know how to dress and play cards…' Fleming was something of a connoisseur of women's fashion, and often describes the clothing of Bond's lovers in lavish detail. The wit is an interesting requirement, since the Bond of the books is never remotely witty: the jokes and one-liners are purely inventions of the films. Fleming uses a great many adjectives to describe the shape of women's breasts most admired by Bond, foremost among which is 'jutting'; this quality, however, is not so attractive when associated with the buttocks, as is the case with Tatiana Romanova's overexercised and therefore unattractively masculine bottom. Elsewhere, confusingly, Fleming approvingly describes a female bottom as 'boyish', a description that sent Noël Coward into a paroxysm of fake-heterosexual outrage: '*Really*, old chap, what could you have been thinking of?' Other critics have got very hot under the collar at Bond's sexual activity: 'Sex, Snobbery and Sadism,' screeched Paul Johnson in the *New Statesman*, blasting the 'mechanical, two-dimensional sex-longings of a frustrated adolescent'.

Fleming worked hard on his seduction technique, but Bond barely needs one: women simply throw themselves at him. Bond Girls are all, of course, intensely attractive, but each bears some small imperfection, a mark of vulnerability: Honeychile Rider has a broken nose; Domino Vitali has one slightly shorter leg. Even their names usually offer the hint of availability, and were often drawn from people Fleming knew: Honeychile was the nickname of Pat Wilder, an American former dancer in Bob Hope's troupe who married Prince Alex Hohenlohe, owner of an exclusive Alpine resort where Fleming went to ski and socialise; Jill Masterton is a play on the name of John Masterman, the Oxford academic who presided over the Double Cross system of double agents during the war; 'Solitaire' (Simone Latrelle in *Live and Let Die*) is named after a unexpectedly dowdy Jamaican bird.

Bond is pure heterosexual, from his brogues to his haircut (which cannot quite be said of Fleming, who had many gay friends and could be fantastically camp). 007 does not approve of homosexuals ('unhappy, sexual misfits') or sexual equality, or even votes for women. His books, Fleming declared, were 'written for warm-blooded heterosexuals'. Outside of the more Jurassic corners of London clubland, it would be hard, these days, to find anyone with the same views as James Bond. 'Doesn't do to get mixed up with neurotic women in this business,' M tells Bond gravely in *From Russia with Love*; 'They hang on to your gun-arm.' All of this adds up to a very potent postwar daydream for a particular sort of old-fashioned gent. Women had the vote and there was nothing even Bond could do about that. Having played a vital role in the war, women were asserting themselves in the home and the workplace; they were even becoming secret agents, and had been effective as such during the war, being rather better in that line of work than men. Male dominance was under threat wherever one looked, but not in Bond's world. Bond offered a reassuring fantasy, old-fashioned in tone but modern in sexual liberty: men were still the world's heroes, modern Saint Georges who could slay the dragon and then fall into the arms of an adoring, beautiful, slightly weak woman, who would love them unquestioningly and then whip up a terrific dinner. Why, he could even cause the toughest lesbian to declare, as does Pussy Galore: 'I never met a man before.'

To many modern men, the Bond Girl myth is still a powerful fantasy; for many modern women, to be called a Bond Girl would be an unforgivable insult. Perhaps that shows that we have not moved on so very far since 1955. Now, woman, where is my Béarnaise sauce?

Ian with Ann Fleming, the woman he married in 1952. Their marriage was complex and often painful, but it was also loving and full of humour.

160

# 007

## SHAKEN, STIRRED AND CUSTOM-MADE: BOND'S LIFE OF LUXURY

## 007
### Shaken, Stirred and Custom-made: Bond's Life of Luxury

'There are moments of great luxury in the life of a secret agent,'
Ian Fleming declared in the opening line of *Live and Let Die* (1954).
It is almost impossible to exaggerate the allure of Bond's lifestyle to
a postwar Britain strained by rationing, deprived of glamour and still
bruised by the privations of war. Bond is, quite simply, a stylish, fast-
shooting, high-living, sexually liberated advertisement for all the
things ordinary Britons had never had, yet dreamed of: the finest
food and drink, smart clothes, fast cars, leisure time, casinos, exotic
foreign travel, swimming in warm waters. Fleming called his evocation
of this fantasy 'disciplined exoticism'. But he was also one of the first
writers to identify the appeal of the designer lifestyle in an emerging
age of consumerism. Identifying Bond with certain brands made him
not only classy, but believable.

Fleming had history on his side, for his dealings in wartime
espionage had shown him that spies do, indeed, enjoy and require
moments of great luxury. Much spycraft is boring, dangerous and
uncomfortable, and spies tend to be self-interested people, fascinated
by material things. Perhaps because of this, human comforts and
luxuries assume a disproportionate importance when an agent is off
duty. John Masterman, organiser of the famed Double Cross system
through which Britain played Germany's spies against their German
spymasters, held it as an article of faith that secret agents should
be pampered and cosseted, provided with money and, within the
bounds of reason and tight security, allowed to indulge themselves
with whatever comforts were available. Popov, the Yugoslavian agent
who spied for Britain throughout the war, was encouraged to live
the life of a gambling, hard-living playboy (not that he needed much
encouragement); Eddie Chapman, codenamed Agent Zigzag, was given
the 'red-carpet treatment' by his MI5 handlers, wined and dined at the
Savoy, and allowed to spend the money he had brought from Germany
on wine, women and, to a slightly lesser extent, song. In framing Bond's
life of exquisite good taste and effortless style, Fleming must surely

ABOVE

Dušan 'Duško' Popov, the
Yugoslavian-born double
agent codenamed 'Tricycle'
who spied for Britain
throughout the war. A man
of expensive tastes and
limitless libido, he was
another inspiration for Bond.

OPPOSITE

Eddie Chapman, aka 'Agent
Zigzag', the British burglar
turned secret agent who
was effectively ordered
to live a life of luxury by his
MI5 handlers, and happily
obliged.

TELEPHONE: GERRARD 7175-6
TELEGRAMS: "SCOTTS" LONDON

SCOTTS

SCOTTS

SCOTTS

TOP OF THE HAYMARKET

OPPOSITE

Scott's, then in the Haymarket, Fleming's favourite restaurant, where he could often be found dining alone on simple dishes such as grilled sole or scrambled eggs.

BELOW

The overcoat worn by Sean Connery over his dinner suit in *Dr No* was deliberately chosen to establish him as a traditionalist. It is a bespoke tailored coat from Anthony Sinclair Ltd of Mayfair.

have been thinking back to the refined wartime spies he had known, like Biffy Dunderdale, who drove around Paris in his Rolls while France collapsed, and dined at Maxim's in his tailor-made suit.

Bond never has to wait in for the electrician or arrange to see the bank manager. He never queues for a bus. In almost every way, his imagined life was entirely divorced from the everyday realities of 1950s Britain. Yet there were people in postwar Britain living a life of exclusive, stylish luxury, and one of them was Ian Fleming. 'I write about what pleasures and stimulates me,' he said, 'and if there is a strong streak of hedonism in my books it is not there by guile but because it comes through the tip of my ball-point pen.'

From an early age, Fleming had enjoyed the good (and expensive) things in life: skiing in the Alps, dining at Scott's, membership of the most exclusive clubs for gentlemen and golfers. For most of his life, however, he did not have quite as much money as he would have liked, and when he did have that kind of money towards the end of his life, having earned vast quantities from his books, it was too late. There is a hunger in the way Fleming describes gold, diamonds, a villain's den or

a delicious meal that transmits itself to the reader as a sort of luxurious longing. Many of his acquaintances were super-rich, most notably his schoolfriend Ivar Bryce, a charming and handsome Anglo-Peruvian sybarite whose already vast family fortune from trading guano was increased immeasurably when he married Jo Hartford, an American supermarket heiress whose fortune was worth an estimated $350 million. The Bryces had homes in, among other places, Manhattan, Vermont, London and the Bahamas (where they had a property complete with a fake beach, imported at $3,000 a yard); they bred racehorses, travelled constantly, partied hard and lived a life of quite breathtaking extravagance. Fleming could be disparaging about the rich, claiming that too much money left millionaires in 'search of identity'; on the other hand, he would have been more than happy with the identity of a multimillionaire himself. His villains are almost all fabulously wealthy: money, and the power it can buy, is central to their evil fascination. 'Too much money is the worst curse you can lay on anyone's head,' Bond tells Marc-Ange Draco in *On Her Majesty's Secret Service*. If so, it was a curse Fleming pursued with consistent determination, and remarkable success.

Fleming was never in the same financial league as the Bryces, but he was still a great deal wealthier than most people, and thanks to a generous expense account provided by Kemsley Newspapers he could live a life that was rather richer than he was. As a young man, he perfected a sort of roué bachelor-chic that lasted throughout his life. He wore suits of the fashionable cut, sported a spotted bow-tie, or the Old Etonian tie ('The colours are really quite unobjectionable'); Fleming considered his tie-wear 'Churchillian'. Churchill did favour spotted black and blue bow-ties (he had only six other ties in the 1950s), which he tied loosely, a style copied precisely by Fleming. Through a long and elegant ebony cigarette holder, Fleming sucked a never-ending succession of custom-made cigarettes. Fleming's smokes were Morland Specials, a tar-heavy confection of strong Turkish and Balkan tobaccos, each one decorated with three gold bands around the filter, in reminiscence of the three gold rings he had worn on his sleeve as (acting) Commander Fleming of the Royal Navy. Bond smokes the same brand, sixty a day and seventy if he is gambling, but when abroad he will smoke whatever the locals are puffing: Chesterfield King Size in the US, Royal Blend in the Caribbean. Fleming's cigarettes were a curious affectation, and a lifelong addiction, but they were also the mark of a man who knew the value of standing out from a crowd. He wore Trumper's 'Eucris' hair dressing (which

Bond also uses in *Diamonds Are Forever*), collected rare books and disdained tea, the working man's drink – Bond declares it 'mud'. Bond's dark suits, Fleming noted with a flash of introspection, 'betray an underlying melancholy'.

On the beach in Jamaica, Bond wears bright beach shirts made by Antonio's of Falmouth, but for everyday wear he sports a blue Sea Island cotton shirt and tropical worsted trousers. Bond and Fleming share most sartorial tastes, although 007 favours black knitted silk ties and would not, I suspect, be seen dead in a spotted bow-tie. Quite how he obtains his wardrobe is a mystery, since Bond goes shopping just once in fourteen books. Little flickers of the more old-fashioned side to Fleming's character occasionally shine through: Bond, for example, takes against anyone wearing a tie knotted in the Windsor style, which he considers 'a mark of vanity, egocentricity and a pawky mind'. (In Red Grant, it is also the mark of an assassin.) Behind Bond the fashion icon lurks Fleming the harrumphing, old-school patriot, disapproving of vulgar dressers, bad manners and homosexuals (even though two of his closest friends, William Plomer and Noël Coward, were gay). Some of Bond's fashion choices would be considered

Noël Coward, Fleming's neighbour in Jamaica and close friend. Coward is owed a debt in the creation of James Bond for persistently badgering Fleming to get on and 'write his bloody book'.

disastrous today, but were then a mark of extreme sophistication, and all reflected Fleming's own idiosyncratic fashion: Bond's taste for pyjama-coats, for example, and black leather sandals (we are not told whether he wears socks with these, but I prefer to assume not).

Fleming's sense of style undoubtedly reflected, in part, his friendship with and admiration for Somerset Maugham. The two writers had met in 1953, when Maugham was already a grand old man of letters, living a life of elegant private luxury in his stunning villa on the Côte d'Azur, with plenty of servants, rare works of art and a sumptuous library. Fleming was deeply impressed by Maugham's expensive English lifestyle.

In some ways Goldeneye, the Jamaican holiday home he purchased in 1946, would become Fleming's answer to Maugham's Villa Mauresque: a haven dedicated to pleasure but also to the hard grind of daily writing. Fleming first visited Jamaica back in 1942, when he travelled there for an Anglo-American naval conference, accompanied by Ivar Bryce. He was immediately smitten by the place. 'When we have won this blasted war, I am going to live in Jamaica,' he declared. 'Just live in Jamaica and lap it up, and swim in the sea and write books.' To another friend he announced that he would never spend another winter in Britain. On the north shore of the island, he found the

By the time Fleming met Somerset Maugham, the older man was already one of the richest and most popular novelists in the world, living a life that combined luxury with literary industry, and which Fleming deeply admired.

property he was looking for, on the site of an old race track, facing the sea, with a secluded private beach. Once more, there was wordplay in the holiday home he called Goldeneye: a reference to the wartime planning for the defence of Gibraltar, Operation Golden Eye, but also a tribute to the Carson McCullers novel *Reflections in a Golden Eye*, which he happened to be reading at the time, and to the original Spanish name of the place, Orcabessa, 'head of gold'. Here Fleming would retreat from the fogs and gloom of wintry London to entertain his friends, snorkel in the warm blue waters of the reef, relax in private luxury and, eventually, write. When it was time to leave this sanctuary in the spring and return home (usually with another finished manuscript in his briefcase), Fleming would always do so with 'a lump in the throat'. Bond would come to share Fleming's deep affection for Jamaica, and in *Live and Let Die* we learn that 007 'had grown to love the great green island and its staunch, humorous people'.

Bond's style is an exaggeration of all the elements that Fleming believed made up the essence of English *savoir-vivre*, with a lot of contemporary consumer goods and designer products thrown in for added glamour. In some respects – most notably food – Bond is far more of a connoisseur than Fleming himself was, but once again he knew instinctively that readers demanded detail. It is not enough to know that Bond wears an expensive watch; we need to know it is a Rolex Oyster Perpetual (although, as Fleming told a reader, he 'has trained himself to tell the time by the sun in either hemisphere within a few minutes'). He does not smoke any old thing (except when abroad), but keeps his Morland cigarettes in a gun-metal case and lights them with a Ronson. He does not simply eat, he eats magnificently and in exquisite detail. Bond's grooming is precise almost to the point of prissiness. His hair is washed in Pinaud Elixir ('that prince among shampoos', he insists, camply), he washes his body with Fleur des Alpes soap by Guerlain, and shaves with a Hoffritz razor. Bond, in short, is a highly perfumed fashion icon, with a licence to smell lovely. 'My books are spattered with branded products of one sort or another', Fleming remarked nonchalantly, but these designer goods are as vital to the man as his machines, his guns or his women.

Bond is a foodie; indeed, he may be the first action-foodie-hero in the thriller genre. Fleming's suggestion that Bond, when not on assignment, often dines simply (grilled sole, *oeufs en cocotte* and the like) stands in sharp contrast to his gastronomic behaviour throughout the series. In *Casino Royale*, Bond declares from the outset: 'I take a ridiculous pleasure in what I eat and drink.' He puts this gourmandising down to being a single man who must often eat alone. Bond's first blow-out, consumed with Vesper Lynd, is worth examining in some detail, for it says much about his tastes (and Fleming's literary intentions). They eat caviar and toast (lots of toast), followed by rare steak tournedos with Béarnaise sauce (so we know what is coming, bed-wise) and artichoke hearts; then Vesper has strawberries and cream, while Bond eats an avocado pear with French dressing. To drink, they have a bottle of the Taittinger Blanc de Brut 1943 – 'probably the finest champagne in the world', Bond muses, and then grins 'at the touch of pretension in the word'.

A touch? To modern ears, this may not sound like a particularly sumptuous meal, but to postwar readers it was almost impossibly recherché and luxurious: a rare, tiny steak when meat itself was rare, usually rubbery and often semi-cremated; an avocado pear was a singularly exotic delicacy – so uncommon, in fact, that Bond seems to think it is a pudding. Champagne is already glamorous enough: the ability not only to spot the difference between one champagne and another, but to declare one to be supreme, that would have been, for Fleming's readers, the mark of true connoisseurship. Pretentious? That was the point: here was a banquet of such immense refinement and expense that readers would be left salivating.

The same is true of many Bond meals. He eats yoghurt in Turkey, but not the low-fat variety; his is 'deep yellow with the consistency of thick cream', and some fresh figs, peeled and 'bursting with ripeness'. This, of course, was in the days before fresh yoghurt could be found in every supermarket in the world. In France, Tilly Masterton is told to buy Bond's lunch: 'Six inches of Lyon sausage, a loaf of bread, and half a litre of Mâcon with the cork pulled.' A bottle of wine with the cork still in it would be merely frustrating, but the precision is the point. Drawing on Fleming's worldwide travels, Bond scoffs every possible gourmet item: lobster in Japan, a doner kebab (then almost unheard of in Britain) in Istanbul, stone crabs and pink champagne from silver tankards in *Goldfinger*, turbot *poché*, *sauce mousseline*, and half a roast partridge from the restaurant opposite the train station in Etaples run by Monsieur Bécaud. For breakfast (his favourite meal, and Fleming's), Bond eats boiled eggs from Maran hens (three and a half minutes each), eaten off Minton china, with toast, Wilkin & Sons Tiptree 'Little Scarlet' strawberry preserve, Frank Cooper's Oxford Vintage Marmalade, honey from Fortnum & Mason, and coffee from De Bry in New Oxford Street, brewed, of course, in the Chemex. The culinary name-dropping is intense: sole meunière, tartare sauce, eggs

Bond's extravagant gastronomic tastes offered a mouthwatering fantasy to postwar readers.

Benedict, thousand island dressing. With M, in the fictional Blades Club, Bond eats asparagus with hollandaise sauce; in Scott's he feasts on lamb cutlets with buttered peas and new potatoes, and a slice of pineapple. To modern, sophisticated palates this is unextraordinary fare, but to contemporaries Bond's meals are bright explosions of high cuisine, specifically designed to tantalise and amaze in a Britain where bananas were considered mouth-wateringly exotic, milk came powdered, and practically everything tasted the same and of very little. In 1948, with control over food supplies even stricter than it had been during the war, the average man was rationed to two ounces of bacon and ham, one and a half ounces of cheese and two ounces of tea each week, and just one egg every five days. The memory of deprivation was still fresh in 1953, and meat rationing would not end until 1954. Bond's diet of asparagus, fresh lamb and pineapple *in a single meal shows* just how far above the average he is.

But here is a small heresy: James Bond might be the ideal comrade in a fight, but in a restaurant he would be sheer hell. Bond would be forever ordering *for* you, offering a little lecture on the wine or champagne, or insisting, as foodies always will, that you cannot eat at the nearest brasserie but must instead trek all the way over to the station in Etaples to try Monsieur Bécaud's divine turbot *poché*. Bond would be the sort to pick a fight with the chef and sommelier. He would forever be on the lookout for Béarnaise sauce. Anyone who insists that food tastes different off Minton china is, in my view, a pain. I am not alone in this. Fleming himself would surely have found Bond a tiresome dining companion: the writer knew the literary value of exotic and complicated foreign food in fiction, but he was no gourmet in fact. Few writers are better at describing food, but eating was not a subject that interested Fleming greatly.

At one point Fleming notes that Bond, when abroad, prefers 'the ordinary plain food of the country'. This was certainly true of Fleming, whose eating habits were closer to M's than to Bond's. His own tastes were straight out of the prep school recipe book. Mostly, he liked scrambled eggs, which 'never let you down', and he did not care much what kind of hen they came from. He insisted that the chef at the Lutèce in New York, then one of the most expensive and exclusive restaurants on the planet, prepare for him scrambled eggs (then strawberries for dessert). Fleming even wrote out his own recipe for scrambled eggs, which offers the artery-clogging suggestion that a meal for four should consist of twelve eggs, six ounces of butter, and additional butter to be stirred in after cooking. However,

Fleming makes scrambled eggs: twelve eggs, lashings of butter, then some more butter. 'I think you sometimes add cream instead of the last piece of butter,' he wrote. Note his unconventional 'hotplate'.

the food Fleming served at Goldeneye – violent goat curries and the like, prepared by his Jamaican housekeeper Violet – was famously revolting, a far cry from the delicacies served by Somerset Maugham at the Villa Mauresque. Noël Coward wrote that 'the food was so abominable I used to cross myself before eating it…it tasted like armpits. And all the time there was old Ian smacking his lips for more and you are tormented by the thought of all those exquisite meals in the books.' Regardless of the quality of the food he served and ate, Fleming was by all accounts a delightful dining companion, entertaining, inquisitive and attentive, particularly if you happened to be an attractive woman. Bond to choose the food and wine, and Fleming to eat it with: that would be the ideal dinner.

'He is basically a hard liquor man,' Fleming said of his fictional creation. 'He is not a wine snob.' Put rather more basically, Bond will drink anything if it is exclusive and sophisticated, and he does, in sometimes quite astonishing quantities. Indeed, his intake of alcohol is so prodigious on occasion that it is amazing he can still stand, let alone shoot straight or make love. In *Moonraker*, before playing cards with Drax, Bond manages to put away a vodka martini, a carafe of vintage vodka from Riga, a bottle of Dom Pérignon champagne and half a packet of the drug Benzedrine. He does not stop there: this is followed by a large brandy and then another entire bottle of champagne. It is something of a relief to discover that Bond is not immune to hangovers. The next morning he vows: 'Champagne and Benzedrine! Never again.' Benzedrine is the trade name for racemic amphetamine, a form of artificial stimulant which causes euphoria, heightens the senses and suppresses the appetite. 'Bennies' were among the first synthetic drugs to be used recreationally, and Benzedrine was used by bomber crews during the Second World War and later by soldiers in the Vietnam War. The socialite 'Chips' Channon used to put it in the cocktails he served during the war, to ensure his parties went with a bang.

In the films, Bond's drinking is essentially pared down to three specific drinks: vodka martinis ('shaken, not stirred'), champagne and whisky on the rocks. In the books, however, his drinking habits are far wider. Bond has a 'head like a rock', according to M, which is just as well given the alcoholic pounding it gets. In *Goldfinger* we find Bond 'luxuriating in the peace and heat of the whisky'. At times, he seems to be less luxuriating in alcohol than marinating in it. As in everything else, Fleming is careful to furnish brand names whenever possible and, like the best barmen, he keeps the drinks coming in a steady stream.

Dom Pérignon, the top champagne of Moët et Chandon. Bond drinks two bottles of the '46 in *Moonraker*, and in the films, Connery, Moore and Lazenby are all partial to this particular label.

young man he brushed shoulders with the so-called Greek Syndicate, a group of ship owners who ran the casino at Deauville. The syndicate's most remarkable dealer was Nicholas Zographos, a character whose stony coolness of temperament matched that of Bond himself. Fleming, unlike Bond, was a cautious gambler, and often an unsuccessful one. Bridge was his game, and although he developed into a good player, he lacked the patience and mathematical precision to master the art beyond amateur competence. At first he played at Boodles, and later at the Portland Club, where the stakes were higher: the two clubs would be amalgamated to form the 'Blades Club' in *Moonraker*, in which Fleming devotes more than sixty pages of intense and vivid description to the game.

Indeed, Fleming became something of an advocate for gambling. For the *Sunday Times* he wrote an article entitled 'How to Win at Roulette with only £10', which was turned down on the grounds that its racy tone might not sit well with the more prim consciences among the newspaper's readership. But it was precisely the sense of indulging in forbidden fruits that gave Bond, the best gambler in the British secret service, such cachet. In journalism, as in fiction, Fleming knew well how to conjure up 'the noisy abracadabra of the roulette table', a heady species of magic most of his readers could barely imagine. By setting scenes in casinos (a literary device borrowed from Somerset Maugham), Fleming transported his readers away from the bomb-scarred cities of Britain to a brighter, sweeter and thrillingly degenerate world. In a semi-serious article for the *Spectator*, entitled 'If I Were Prime Minister' (a fairly alarming proposition), Fleming suggested that the Isle of Wight be turned into a huge pleasure island, where 'frustrated citizens of every class could give rein to the basic instincts for sex and gambling which have been crushed through the ages'. (Given his earlier suggestion that the Isle of Wight be made French during the war, one wonders what Fleming had against this blameless island.)

Fleming's other main recreational hobby was golf. It may seem strange, in an age when golf is one of the most democratic and widely played games in the world, that at the time when Bond was first climbing into his plus-fours the sport held a peculiar, elite glamour. Fleming first played golf with his grandmother, took up the game at prep school, and played until the end of his life (indeed, a cold caught playing golf led to his final illness). It was a game that gave him the purest and simplest pleasure, and most weekends he could be found on one of Britain's courses: Gleneagles, Cooden in Sussex, and most famously at Royal Saint George's in Kent, which would become the

A memento from Ian Fleming's visit to Las Vegas in 1959. The writer loved to gamble, and relished the atmosphere of casinos, but unlike Bond he bet cautiously, and often lost.

OPPOSITE

Bond in the bunker:
Ian Fleming playing golf.


BELOW

The shoes worn by Auric
Goldfinger (Gert Fröbe)
in *Goldfinger* (1964).
The golf scenes were shot
at Stoke Poges Golf Club
in Buckinghamshire in May
1964.

fictional Royal Saint Mark's in *Goldfinger*. Golf offered Fleming the
sort of male companionship he often craved, the opportunity to spend
a few hours in the open air with some like-minded, clubbable friends, a
modicum of exercise followed by an immodicum of drinks. Once again,
his enthusiasm outpaced his ability: he played off a handicap of nine
(so does Bond), but developed an inhibiting 'flat swing' (so does Bond).
Agent 007 is happy to cheat his way to victory in *Goldfinger*, something
his creator would never have done (even if his opponent was already
doing so), but Fleming was also happy to gamble on the outcome:
when he was young, the bet was a mere £1; as he grew older and
richer, the stakes rose to a hefty £50 a round or more. Fleming never
became a golf bore, because while he was passionate about the game
he never took it too seriously. Sometimes the wager was frivolous –
say, a pair of monogrammed pyjamas. He scandalised the stuffier
members of the Old Etonian Golfing Society by presenting it with an
unusual prize cup: a chamber pot inscribed with the words 'The James
Bond All Purpose Grand Challenge Vase'. He was also capable of mocking
his own golfing pretensions, as in an article entitled 'Nightmare among
the Mighty' which he wrote for the *Sunday Times* about his participation
and unexpected success in a pro-celebrity tournament.

Fleming with the sort of suggestion that newspaper editors, in my experience, never make: would Fleming care to take a five-week, all-expenses-paid trip around the world, to visit the globe's most thrilling cities? Astonishingly, Fleming apparently needed persuading to take up this offer. 'Surely you want to pick up some material for your stories,' said Russell. 'It's a wonderful opportunity.'

Fleming's 'Thrilling Cities' world tour in 1959 was a remarkable odyssey. The first leg took him to Hong Kong ('modern comfort in a theatrically oriental setting'), Macau, to gamble in a nine-storey house of pleasure, and to Tokyo, where he composed haikus with geisha girls. In Hong Kong he linked up with the *Sunday Times* Asia correspondent, Richard Hughes, a large and ebullient Australian (and part-time spy) who was doyen of the city's foreign press corps, and in Tokyo he was guided by another journalist, 'Tiger' Saito. As with Nazim Kalkavan, his Turkish guide to Istanbul in 1956, Fleming would repay his local guides by granting them immortality in *You Only Live Twice*, as Richard Lovelace 'Dikko' Henderson, the Australian stationed in Japan, and Tiger Tanaka, the head of the Japanese secret service. Fleming was no culture-vulture; his requirements were entertainment, comfort and colour: 'No politicians, museums, temples, Imperial palaces or Noh plays, let

A collection of Fleming's Japanese travel brochures. The writer travelled widely during the war, and after it, gathering material for his novels and relentlessly pursuing new and exotic locations.

alone tea ceremonies.' He wanted to experience casinos, restaurants and brothels, the high life, night life and low life, the glamour and, of course, the girls: 'In the East, sex is a delightful pastime totally unconnected with sin,' he declared. But then, sin had never been much of a preoccupation for Fleming.

The plane from Tokyo to Hawaii caught fire and nearly crashed. In Los Angeles, he visited the head of police intelligence to bone up on the local mafia scene, and in Las Vegas he made $100 on the slot machines and stole three ashtrays as souvenirs. In Chicago, he broke his own no-museums rule and visited that city's fine collection of Impressionist art, but he also found time to see a striptease ('positively exquisite boredom') and the site of the St Valentine's Day Massacre. New York, his final destination and a city he had always loved, proved, on this occasion, to be a disappointment, no doubt compounded by travel fatigue after more than a month on the road and his mounting ill health. Fleming complained that the city was in thrall to television and tranquillisers, and in a later Bond short story he grumbled that the best restaurants had been colonised by a new 'expense account aristocracy' – a criticism which, given his own elevated position within that particular caste, was pretty rich. Some of this jaundiced attitude to America would reappear in *You Only Live Twice*, when Bond reflects on Britain's fast-diminishing global role and Tiger Tanaka hits out at the new American superpower dominating East and West: 'Baseball, amusement arcades, hot dogs, hideously large bosoms, neon lightings.' Just a few months later, Fleming would repeat the 'Thrilling Cities' experience with a whistle-stop canter through selected European cities, including Hamburg, Berlin, Vienna, Geneva (where he met Charlie Chaplin) and Monte Carlo.

These trips would result in a successful and popular newspaper series covering thirteen cities in all. 'Thrilling Cities' was published in book form in 1963, but beyond that the extended double journey furnished Fleming with vast amounts of contemporary material for his novels. Ann remarked acidly that she did not see how Ian could be thrilled by any city, since he never stayed long enough to see anything. But that was the way Ian travelled, Fleming wrote and Bond lived: impressionistically, thrillingly and very fast.

Travel, golf, swimming, gambling, reading, book-collecting: these were all, to some extent, the habits of a solitary man. The boy who had eschewed team games at Eton in favour of athletics remained a solo player all his life. The character traits that made him shy away from commitment to women were also those that drove him to pursue, alone, the things that most fascinated him. This surely also explains why, in that explosion of creativity in the last years of his life, he was able to devote himself utterly to the most solitary and lonely occupation of all: writing.

Bond's lifestyle echoed and exaggerated that of his creator, perhaps to a greater extent than any other twentieth-century writer, though the parallels are far from perfect. Bond is a superb shot, whereas Fleming hated shooting, and did it as seldom as he could. Bond exercises daily, and retains his fitness despite his habits, while the summit of Fleming's health regime was swimming or an amble around the golf course. Fleming was an avid reader, book collector and bibliophile; Bond's bookshelves are apparently full, but there is little evidence he has ever read the books therein. Indeed, books are hardly mentioned in Bond's world, save for a few, including *Hogan on Golf*, *Scarne on Cards* and a few books written (inevitably) by Fleming's friends: Raymond Chandler, Eric Ambler and Patrick Leigh Fermor, as well as JFK's *Profiles in Courage*. Bond lives in Chelsea and never has the slightest money worries; Fleming, until the final chapter of his life, never had quite enough cash. Bond reads *The Times*, every day; Fleming, a journalist to his core, read every newspaper and magazine he could lay his hands on. Bond is childless and parentless; Fleming had a complex relationship with his mother, and strove to be a good father to his only son, Caspar. Fleming was brought up in an age where children were to be seen and not heard; in Bond's life they are neither seen nor heard.

Fleming had not intended to give James Bond a style. He was to be a blunt instrument, an empty vessel. But in the end, in spite of himself, Bond's way of life and way of thinking were broadly those of Fleming. Above all, Fleming and Bond share an interest in things, the rarer and more exclusive the better. In this, both writer and creation were harbingers of a new consumer age, when lifestyle and fashion would matter increasingly, and the label often proclaimed the man. 'We are the only two writers,' Fleming told Somerset Maugham, 'who write about what people are really interested in: cards, money, gold and things like that.' Bond admits, almost sheepishly, to taking a 'ridiculous' interest in food, drink and other material things. But Fleming knew exactly what he was doing. The writing technique he pioneered was far from being ridiculous, and very close to being inspired.

Fleming was among the first novelists to mention specific products in his books, particularly luxury brands, to the delight of their manufacturers.

FLORIS

By Appointment, J. Floris Ltd., Perfumers to the late King George VI

# FLORIS

ESTABLISHED 1730

89 JERMYN STREET, LONDON, S.W.1

TELEGRAPHIC ADDRESS: FLORISSIMA PICCY LONDON
TELEPHONES: WHITEHALL 2885 AND 4136

Ian Fleming, Esq.,
c/o Messrs. Jonathan Cape Ltd.          17th
30, Bedford Square,                      April
LONDON. W.C.1.                           1958.

Dear Sir,

        May the writer, on behalf of
this firm, acknowledge your kind mention
of "Floris" in your latest book "Doctor No".

        May he also wish your book the
very great success it deserves, and he
would appreciate it if you would kindly
accept the enclosed bottle of Limes Bath
Essence with Messrs. Floris' compliments
and thanks.

                Yours faithfully,
                    p.p. J. FLORIS LTD.

Enc: 1 Limes Bath Essence.

# 008

## THE SHORT LIFE OF
## IAN FLEMING;
## THE ETERNAL LIFE OF
## JAMES BOND

## 008
### The Short Life of Ian Fleming; The Eternal Life of James Bond

By 1961, and the publication of *Thunderball*, James Bond is ailing. As the book opens, he wakes up feeling dreadful, chronically hungover. Boredom, and the soft life he has always feared, are taking their toll. M dispatches him to a health farm, Shrublands, where the medical report is stern. 'The officer's daily consumption of alcohol is in the region of half a bottle of spirits of between sixty and seventy proof,' the doctor writes. 'The tongue is furred. The blood pressure a little raised at 160/90…the officer admits to frequent occipital headaches.' The report blames Bond's habits: 'I believe these symptoms are due to the officer's mode of life. He is not responsive to the suggestion that over-indulgence is no remedy for the tensions inherent in his professional calling…'

Fleming's report on the health of his hero was broadly autobiographical: the drinking, high blood pressure and headaches were all symptoms suffered with increasing persistence by the writer himself. In Bond's refusal to countenance changing his unhealthy and indulgent lifestyle, Fleming was stating his own determination not to waste his life by trying to extend it. Yet he was aware that his body was failing. Shrublands is based on Enton Hall, an expensive and exclusive health farm, or 'hydro', in Surrey. Ann Fleming had visited Enton Hall, and she persuaded Ian to book into the health farm to treat his painful sciatica, headaches and generally failing health. He did not enjoy the strict regime, and scoffed at the faddish nature remedies prescribed. His doctor prescribed more pills.

For all his vigour, Fleming had never enjoyed robust good health. The shadow of mortality was seldom far behind him, and in a notebook he wrote with wry candour: 'I've always had one foot not wanting to leave the cradle, and the other in a hurry to enter the grave, which has made for an uncomfortable existence.' Fleming was just thirty-eight when he first began to suffer serious chest pains, which spread to his neck. A New York medical specialist told him to cut down on the cigarettes and drink, advice that he would continue to receive, and fail

Fleming smoked custom-made Morland Specials, each one decorated with three gold bands in memory of the rings on the sleeves of his wartime naval uniform. He smoked elegantly, constantly and fatally.

to heed, for the rest of his life. He suffered from stress and persistent headaches – possibly a legacy from his broken and ill-mended nose. A cardiogram in 1949 showed no evidence of heart disease, but in retrospect what Fleming called the 'iron crab' had plainly already taken a grip on his heart. In 1956, he was struck down by agonising kidney stones, which would develop into another recurrent problem. Soon after the publication of *Thunderball* in 1961, Fleming suffered a major heart attack and spent a month in hospital, followed by a long convalescence at a hotel on the coast near Brighton. He was put on a strict diet, which he tried to circumvent by sneaking in smoked salmon and other forbidden delicacies. He also began writing *Chitty Chitty Bang Bang*, based on the bedtime stories he would tell his son Caspar. 'There is not a moment even on the edge of the tomb,' he told his publisher, 'when I am not slaving for you.'

He joked that Ann was trying to convince him that 'going for long walks and looking for birds' nests is the right way to spend the next forty years of my life'. Fleming had just three years of life left, and for all his grim joviality, he probably knew it. Blanche Blackwell, his lover in the final few years, noted that he was 'fighting like a tiger to live, but everything was against it'. *Thunderball* opens on a bleak note: 'It was one of those days when it seemed to James Bond that all life, as someone put it, was nothing but a heap of six to four against.' For Fleming, the odds on his own life expectancy were steadily getting worse, but at the very moment when his books were about to hit the most astonishing winning streak.

When describing his writing methods, Fleming reached for a water-sports metaphor: 'Each chapter is like a wave to be jumped as we race behind the hero like a water-skier behind a fast motor boat.' Forcing the reader to turn the page was the only rule of thriller-writing that mattered, and he stuck to the formula religiously, writing at the pace of the most daredevil water-skier, but with iron discipline. Over the course of fourteen years, every one of the Bond novels was written in Goldeneye as winter turned to spring, usually taking about eight weeks, and then published a year later: two thousand words every morning between 9.30 and 12.30, or approximately seven hundred words an hour. 'If you interrupt the writing of fast narrative with too much introspection and self-criticism, you will be lucky to write five hundred words a day,' he advised.

There spoke the true journalist. Unsurprisingly, he sometimes made mistakes: occasionally the plot blows a gasket, and screeches to

*Chitty Chitty Bang Bang: The Magical Car*, the children's book Fleming wrote for his son Caspar, which was first published in 1964. Four years later, Pan released this paperback edition, tying in with the highly successful film starring Dick Van Dyke and Sally Ann Howes.

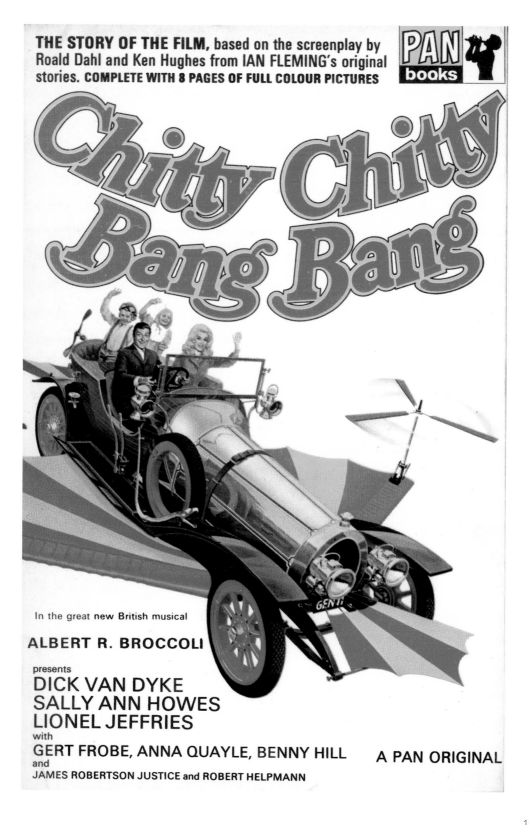

a halt; sometimes the narrative flags; and the later Bond books lack some of the brio of the early novels. But for the most part, the books sail along with infectious verve and confidence. Returning to England with a completed manuscript, Fleming would then set to work correcting the proofs of the book written the previous spring, before starting to cook up a fresh plot, with new experts and fresh opportunities for travel. It was a hurtling rhythm of work, and it translated into a breathless, heart-thumping style. For Fleming, the demands were exhilarating, exhausting and relentless. He seldom rewrote in any substantial way: the books seemed to flow from him almost fully formed, on the initial draft. The first people to see the manuscript would be William Plomer, Fleming's old friend and his most loyal and reliable critic, and his brother, Peter. The self-deprecation continued: 'My books are straight pillow-book fantasies of the bang-bang kiss-kiss variety,' Fleming declared, with that appealing nonchalance. This was simply untrue. Fleming had discovered an extraordinary recipe, and the public, if not always the critics, recognised it as such.

The reviewers, at least initially, were gentle with James Bond. When not plugging the work of his friends in newspapers or novels, Ian was an avid and expert self-promoter, and as a senior newspaperman he was in a position to ensure some favourable notices; yet the rave reviews were more than mere log-rolling. With the publication of *Casino Royale*, the *Sunday Times*, his own newspaper, hailed Ian Fleming as 'the best new thriller-writer since Eric Ambler'. But other newspapers, which might have been expected to be more impartial or even hostile, were equally enthusiastic: 'Ian Fleming has discovered the secret of narrative art,' declared John Betjeman in the *Daily Telegraph*. 'Don't miss this,' advised the *Observer*. Even the *Times Literary Supplement*, bible of the higher-browed, proclaimed: 'Mr Fleming has produced a book that is both exciting and extremely civilised.' Amid all the plaudits, however, one can already detect the early rumblings of the backlash that would eventually follow. One reviewer considered the scenes of torture in *Casino Royale* 'too monstrous to be excused'. Another recommended that Fleming 'cut down on the physical violence'. The reaction to the US publication was also somewhat muted. In one of the more remarkably askew assessments in literary history, one reviewer insisted that this British secret agent was 'passé'.

The first print run of *Casino Royale*, 4,750 books, sold out in a month. Jonathan Cape, the publisher, had not expected much from the book, and agreed to accept it for publication only after Peter Fleming, an established author, interceded on his brother's behalf. 'He's got to do much better if he's going to get anywhere near Peter's standard,' Cape remarked. But with *Casino Royale* selling well, Cape offered Fleming a contract for three further books, and his career as a novelist was well and truly launched. James Bond, as ever, provoked different reactions: some serious-minded critics baulked at the implausibility; others squirmed at the sex and violence; a few resented the brand-naming and what looked like product placement, as it has since become known. But Fleming also found supporters in the most unlikely and useful places. He had been introduced to Raymond Chandler at a luncheon party given by the poet Stephen Spender. The acclaimed master of the American detective novel would prove a loyal fan, reviewing both *Diamonds Are Forever* (apparently his first ever review) and *Dr No*, and declaring Fleming to be 'probably the most forceful and driving writer of what I suppose still must be called thrillers in England'.

Sales were good, but nowhere near what they would become, or what Fleming would like them to have been. Some of Fleming's early success may be ascribed to canny promotion, and some to mere good luck. If *Live and Let Die* had been entitled *The Undertaker's Wind*, as Fleming originally planned, then one wonders if the entire Bond series might have come to a premature end. Reviews for the first five books were, on balance, positive. In Fleming's own words, 'the great thing is that each one of the books seems to have been a favourite with one or another section of the public, and none has yet been completely damned'.

Damnation, swiftly followed by the breakthrough Fleming craved, would come in 1958 with the publication of *Dr No*. The critics rounded on Fleming, almost as a pack, and Bond-bashing became the order of the day. Fleming's writing was pilloried as vulgar, licentious and immoral, snobbish and anachronistic, with a nasty flavour of sado-masochism. The most famous assault came from Paul Johnson in the *Spectator*, who claimed that Bond had been cooked up from three base ingredients: 'all unhealthy, all thoroughly English – the sadism of the school bully, the mechanical two-dimensional sex-longings of a frustrated adolescent, and the crude, snob-cravings of a suburban adult'. The London literary cognoscenti had always looked down on Bond, even, most painfully for Fleming, his own wife Ann and her coterie of writers and intellectuals, which included such luminaries as Evelyn Waugh and Peter Quennell. Ann could be particularly withering, refusing to allow him to dedicate *Casino Royale* to her on the grounds that 'books of this sort' (i.e. cheap ones) do not merit dedications. 'I would so love him to triumph over the sneers of Annie's intellectual friends,' observed Noël Coward. And triumph he did. The attacks reflected the fact that Fleming was now well known enough to warrant being attacked: helped by the notoriety and controversy, the faint but exciting whiff of immorality and sexual mischief, the Bond books acquired their own momentum. The critics continued to complain, often savagely; the readers, too, were sometimes angered when Fleming appeared to tinker with the established formula, as in *The Spy Who Loved Me*, narrated by the fictional Vivienne Michel. But Bond was becoming unstoppable. In 1959, *Goldfinger* hurtled directly to the top of the best-seller lists.

Fleming knew the value of a plot twist, but nothing could have prepared him for the change in Bond's fortunes that would occur when 007 finally transferred to the movie screen. In October 1962, Fleming attended the film premiere of *Dr No*, the first instalment in what would become the most valuable cinematic franchise in history. Bond, for better and for worse, would never be the same again. Nor would he ever again be solely the product of Fleming's imagination. For many people, James Bond is a film character (or several film characters), but his path to the screen had not been simple or swift. Fleming had always intended that his creation should transfer to film or television, and as with the books, he worked hard to bring about the transformation.

This was less easy than, with hindsight, might have been expected. The rights to *Casino Royale* were sold to CBS in 1954 for $1,000 and later adapted into a television play as part of a series entitled *Climax*, now almost wholly forgotten. Sir Alexander Korda, the great Hungarian-born producer, toyed with the idea of making *Live and Let Die*, but the idea came to nothing. In 1958, Fleming was commissioned to write a thirteen-part Bond series, again for CBS in the US. Once again, the project foundered, but much of the material Fleming had written would be recycled in different forms in the later books. Like many writers, Fleming was frustrated by Hollywood's capacity for encouraging talk and no action: 'hollow bonhomie combined with ultra-sharp horse-trading' was how he put it. Yet he persevered, and set out to create a film project of his own. Through Ivar Bryce, he met an up-and-coming filmmaker, Kevin McClory, and together (along with screenwriter Jack Whittingham) they set about writing a treatment for an underwater Bond adventure set in the Caribbean. Once again, the project foundered, mainly for lack of financial backing, but as usual Fleming was unwilling to see hard work go to waste and adapted the idea into the novel *Thunderball*. This time, however, the recycling got him into serious trouble, when McClory and Whittingham claimed the book was based partly on their

Film director Terence Young,
on whom Sean Connery
partly based his
characterisation of Bond,
with Connery and Molly
Peters on the set of
*Thunderball*. Bond would
never have worn a hat in bed.

OVERLEAF
Ian Fleming with Ursula
Andress and Sean Connery
on the set of *Dr No*.

work and sued in the High Court for breach of copyright. The resulting legal wrangle was bitter, intensely complex and, for Fleming, quite debilitating; it would not be resolved for a further thirty-seven years. At one point in the process, he was reduced to drawing up a list of the ideas, details and inspirations that he had put into the book, in order to back up his claim to sole authorship. This legal document again demonstrated both the depth and eclecticism of Fleming's research: the specifications for the *Disco Volante*, for example, had been obtained from the Italian boat manufacturer Leopoldo Rodriguez; the title *Thunderball* came from a conversation in which Fleming had heard this term used to describe an American atomic test; and so on. For later archaeologists of the Bond phenomenon, such details are fascinating; for Fleming, forced to pick apart his own writing in order to prove ownership, the entire legal experience was hellish. His first heart attack came just two weeks after the court action was launched. 'I do not think James Bond would be at home in the Chancery Division,' Fleming observed morosely as the case dragged on.

Film salvation arrived in the somewhat unlikely double act of Albert Romolo 'Cubby' Broccoli, an experienced Italian-American Hollywood producer, and Harry Saltzman, a Canadian former circus

performer and intelligence agent turned movie impresario. Saltzman had acquired the film rights to all the Bond books (save *Casino Royale*), and in partnership with Broccoli he founded EON Productions – standing for Everything Or Nothing – which was a good motto for their high-stakes gambling style. United Artists signed up to make six films, with Fleming earning an impressive $100,000 per film and 5 per cent of producer's profits. Broccoli and Saltzman decided to open the franchise with *Dr No*, which has arguably the most filmic of the Bond villains. Bond was about to hit the big time on the big screen, but Fleming's control over the character, inevitably, would begin to diminish.

It is said that Fleming initially wanted the part of Dr Julius No to be played by Noël Coward, his old friend and neighbour in Jamaica, a prospect that would have been hilarious, and probably disastrous. He also suggested that David Niven, another friend, should play Bond, or Richard Burton, whom he much admired, or else a young actor named Roger Moore. Ian's suggestions were politely ignored, though in private Broccoli could be less than flattering about the novelist's work: *Dr No*, he allegedly said to one potential director, was 'full of nonsense'. Cary Grant was initially offered the part of Bond, but at fifty-eight he declined, reportedly saying he was too old for the role. Eventually Broccoli decided to cast Sean Connery, an almost entirely unknown Scottish actor who had previously worked as a truck-driver, life-class model, milkman, coffin polisher, sailor, boxer and lifeguard. Fleming had lunch with Connery at the Savoy, but wondered if this Scottish working-class 'overgrown stuntman' was quite right for the part. His doubts were allayed when an attractive woman at the same lunch assured him that Connery had 'it', the indefinable sex appeal that would work on screen. Even if he had objected, it is doubtful whether Fleming's opinion would have made much difference: under the terms of the contract, he had no influence over or input into the scripts. In any case, as screenwriter Richard Maibaum conceded, there was an 'untransferable quality' in the novels. Fleming's role was restricted to scouting film locations in Jamaica, but there is no evidence he minded: like many sensible authors, he decided to bank the cheque, stand in the wings and watch the action from a discreet distance.

Even so, Fleming became predictably fascinated by the mechanics of film-making, and he had a clear notion of how Bond should be presented on screen. As in the books, he believed Bond should be depicted as a 'blunt instrument wielded by a government department', a cog in a 'tough, modern organisation', and not particularly appealing 'until [the audience] get to know him and then they will appreciate

*Fleming on the set of*
*Goldfinger* with Sean
Connery and Shirley Eaton.

while Charlie Higson successfully took on the challenge of writing the Young Bond series, and Samantha Weinberg took the myth in another direction with *The Moneypenny Diaries*. The novelist Sebastian Faulks has now joined the party, with the latest authorised Bond novel, *Devil May Care*, published to mark the centenary of Fleming's birth.

One might expect Ian Fleming himself to have become lost in the huge branding and marketing industry that is James Bond, but he is still there, in the firm jaw of his hero, the punchy prose, the style, the love of things and the sheer craftsmanship of the original writing. He is there, too, in the peculiar mixture of reality and fantasy that is the essence of the Bond books, and the reason for their enduring appeal. Few novelists have given so much pleasure, for so long. Mention the name James Bond to almost anyone, anywhere, and they will smile. Many writers now do what Fleming first did, but nobody does it better. One hundred years after Ian Fleming's birth, James Bond is fifty-six, the precise age that Fleming was when he died, much too young. But 007 is still young, and ageless.

The door to M's office: behind this Bond gets his orders, his next assignment and, as often as not, a stern ticking-off.

OVERLEAF
Ian Fleming with film producer Harry Saltzman on the set of *Dr No*.

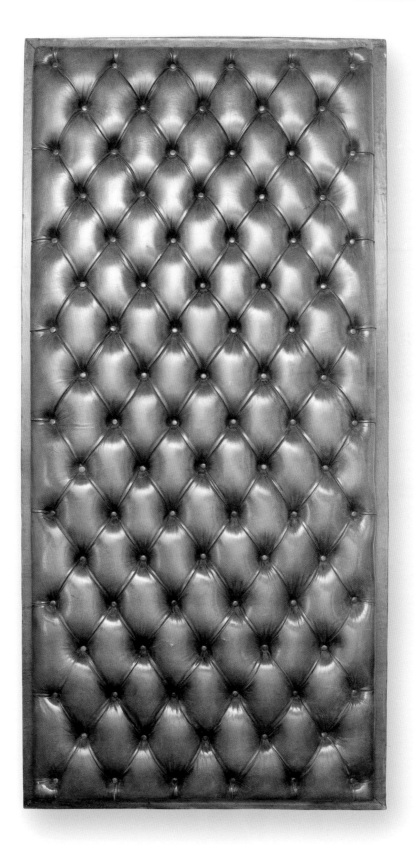